101 AWESOME THINGS TO DO *for Someone Who's Sick*

Caring Ideas + Resources + Gifts + Stories + Love

ELAINE WILKES, PhD

Available in e-Book and print editions. For special discounts on bulk purchases, send inquiries to: Elaine@ElaineWilkes.com.

DISCLAIMER:
The author of this book does not dispense medical advice or prescribe the use of any technique as a form of treatment, either directly or indirectly. The intent of the author is only to offer information of a general nature to help you in your quest for helping yourself or sick ones. In the event you, or anyone you know, use any of the information in this book for yourself, or for others, which is your constitutional right, the author and the publisher assume no responsibility for your actions.

Photo Credits:
Front cover photo: iStockPhoto.com
Pictures used in the stories are either from iStockPhoto, or the contributor of the story.
Hope in Bloom photo credits: Roberta Dehman Hershon

Note: Everything is strictly for information purposes only, and the author, or anyone associated with this book, are not liable for any use of the products or services listed.

"Those among you
who will be really happy
are those who will have
sought and found how to serve."

—Albert Schweitzer

About This Book

I had two family members hospitalized in critical care at the same time.

Each day, as I walked down long, sterile hospital hallways, I noticed patients who looked lonely, depressed, or bored, and as a result time seemed to d-r-a-g on for them.

Geez, I didn't want that for my family. So what could I do? Most of us have been in this same predicament of wanting to do something to show we care, but many times we don't know what.

So I started searching for ideas, but I couldn't find anything that was really helpful and awesome.

I began asking people from all over the world for the most loving, rewarding, fun, or helpful things they've done for sick family members, friends, or even strangers.

People opened their hearts with touching stories that are beyond helpful, and totally awesome. If you've ever wondered what you can do that's meaningful for someone who's sick, then this easy-read is for you!

This book is filled with proven suggestions that have helped or brightened someone's life. Many of the simple acts of kindness sprinkled throughout this book are so appreciated they will be cherished in their memories forever.

You'll also discover invaluable services that most people don't even know exist that greatly help people who are ill.

How to Use This Book:

This valuable information is grouped into the following categories:

1. Inspiring Stories
2. The Loving Side of Technology
3. Awesome Ideas For Caregivers and Advocates
4. Tasty Food Ideas
5. Practical, Easy, Helpful Ideas
6. Making it Super Special (Takes More Time)
7. Nurturing Ideas
8. Emotional Support
9. Great Gift Ideas
10. Ideas from Patients
11. Final Thoughts

At the end of the book you'll find websites and information about the people who shared their ideas and stories. **Some offer coupon codes for discounts.**

Since writing *101 Awesome Things for Someone Who is Sick,* my family members returned home, recovered, and are doing great.

Please see more awesome stuff on www.facebook.com/101AwesomeThings

Contents

"When adversity strikes, be calm.
Take a step back, stay strong,
stay grounded and press on."

— LL Cool J

Awesome Ideas From Inspiring Stories

"Through every obstacle exists an opportunity for transformational change."

- John Douillard

Stay In the Now

"When you can think of yesterday without regret and tomorrow without fear, you are near contentment."
— Source Unknown

Several years ago, my husband fell from a ladder doing a household project and suffered a serious brain injury.

From the first day in the hospital, my sons and I knew our lives would never be the same. My husband was unconscious in the ICU for almost a month and the doctors didn't know if he would make it.

Thankfully he pulled through, began to improve, went to a rehab, and later finally came home.

My advice to anyone facing a similar situation is to not let your mind think about the future.

Take every day as it comes.

You waste a lot of energy when you start worrying about what will happen next month or next year, or in 10 years.

Stay in the moment and let go of the past (how things were before) and the future (what will happen to me) and concentrate on what is occurring . . . NOW.

– Laura Ellison Cook

Bring Them Into Nature

My hospice patient was a 45 year-old trucker waiting to die. He had spent much of his life outside and felt trapped, as he was confined to bed, due to his pain at the end stages of his disease.

His greatest wish, to go outside again, was undo-able. He couldn't even tolerate sitting in a wheelchair. His sadness was profound and palpable, so I decided I was gonna make it happen.

I got a portable oxygen tank, hooked him up, released the brakes on his bed and we rolled down the hall!

With his family helping push the bed, we took him out the ER doors, through the parking lot and settled him beneath a shady tree.

He was ecstatic to be outside again, to feel the wind in his face and to breathe the fresh air. He was content relaxing and chatting with his family there for several hours.

It was the last time he was able to get outside as he died a few days later.

I know that I assisted this man to have a peaceful passing and was able to give him and his family a few hours that weren't focused on pain and suffering.

– Brenda Schetnan,
RN, Awesome Hospice Nurse

Awesome Thing to Do!

Get out in nature. It's like a reset button for your brain and emotions.

Mow Their Lawn

When my baby was in the hospital (four hours from our home) for his second open-heart surgery in seven months, one of my neighbors came and mowed our yard (2/3 of an acre!), so that when we came home, we didn't have to walk through a jungle.

I never found out who did it; they never stepped forward even when I asked others about it. I think I know who did it, but I can't be quite sure.

Having our yard cut meant our home looked even MORE welcoming after a month's stay in the hospital. I'll always remember that act as one of the great kindnesses shown to my family during a most difficult time.

– *Anna Jaworski,*
Author

Serenade Them

As the story goes, my dad, Colman, was an amazing singing talent in his younger years.

While in an Illinois airport, my father had a quadruple heart attack. He had gone into the men's room to freshen up when he leaned over the sink, almost fainting. A female janitor came into the room and asked if he was okay. She insisted on bringing in the airport security.

They rushed him to a local hospital and immediately into surgery.

After surgery, my dad wanted to thank the female janitor, only to find that this particular airport did not have any female janitors. My dad told his story to the airport staff, again only to have them repeat there were no female janitors on staff. We believe it was an angel acting on his behalf.

Every day he was getting worse.

Finally, my father who was a world-renowned

singer and orator just decided to stop speaking. He could no longer sing, he was barely able to move without a walker, and all he did was shake his head yes or no.

His doctor, Dr. Varig Shah, knowing dad so well, and the history of his career, prescribed something special for dad in the hospital.

Mother and I were heading down to the cafeteria for dinner. As mom and I were leaving his room, I noticed a gentleman, looking very much like a younger version of my dad, walking down the hospital hallway with a guitar on his back. I made a comment that it was a wonderful gesture from a volunteer, until I noticed he went straight into my father's room. Mom and I turned around, going back to see what he was up to.

He greeted dad and started to strum his guitar. The tune sounded vaguely familiar. To my amazement, he had learned all of the songs that my father was known for in his heyday.

My father, who had not opened his mouth in over six months, joined this young man in song. My dad's face lit up, there was a light, long gone in his eyes, and his voice was as strong and clear as it had once been.

I stood in my father's room—and cried.

Dr. Shah had given this young man some of dad's old CD's and asked him to learn a couple of songs to sing with my father.

I wish that I could say there's a happy ending, but that was the last time I heard my father really sing.

–Tammye McDuff [Dunn]

Give Them a "Celebrity" Visit

I was 10 years old and had undergone surgery, which involved breaking my sternum and detaching it from my ribs.

A few days later, lying in the hospital bed, I was drifting in and out of a sleepy daze while my parents tried to feed me. Though the medication had mostly worn off, there still seemed to be a fog in the room.

As I stared at the open doorway wondering how long it would be before I could pass through it and go home, in bound a tall, handsome, smiling man with a stuffed animal under each arm. I immediately recognized my hero, baseball southpaw Frank Tanana, standing next to the bed. "Heyyyyyy Kay-Kayyy!! How're they treating you!" His words were bright, big and full of life.

My heart raced underneath the bandages. He sat on the bed next to mine and put the animals on the empty food tray. More palpitations. I laughed at an earth-colored googly-eyed owl made of puffy yarn and a smiling grey angora cat with a red felt heart.

Realizing that my dad had asked him to come, I lay there grinning and giggling, not wanting to be anywhere else.

He stayed for about 20 minutes, but those animals became treasures for years to come. Each time I touched them I remembered how his kindness touched me. And how special it made me feel.

–Karen Seeberg,
Spiritual guidance counselor

Be a Watchdog with Complications and Insurance

I woke up after being in a coma for 20 days and was stunned to hear that my left leg would have to be amputated above the knee, my right leg below the knee, and I'd lose the thumb and two fingers of my left hand.

I could use only one hand after the amputations, but the nurse said she couldn't help me eat because they were understaffed. Fortunately my husband could help me at lunch and dinner.

I was moved to another facility, but situation was the same. I don't know if this is a nationwide problem, but my needs were ignored. I was there five long months. Finally, I was able to eat with one hand.

Every few days I would ask for a shampoo cap (it's to wash hair without water). I never even received a bath.

I was taken to physical therapy for 15 minutes a

day, which was a joke since I had didn't have legs! I wanted desperately to get out of there even though I couldn't move, and could only use one hand.

One day my thoughtful daughter somehow managed to get me into a wheelchair and over to the bathroom sink. After seven weeks, with her help, I got my first shampoo! However, all the chemicals and medicines I received, plus lying on my back for so long, caused me to lose all my hair!

I moved to a third facility and finally got my first shower. I was there for two weeks, but still didn't have my artificial legs.

When I informed them I still had stitches on the stump of my left leg they replied, "No, no, they'll dissolve, and you can go home." But, when they saw I couldn't sit on the toilet, they sent me to a nursing home.

I was in the nursing home for two months. I told them I still had stitches in my leg, and it looked infected. They said it was just red from the scar, and the doctor would check me in a week. Finally, strings started popping out of my leg followed by puss.

I insisted I see the surgeon. Going to his office was a huge undertaking without limbs and use only of one hand. He said he didn't know which leg the knots were on!

Ten days later I was back in ER and was operated on again because the skin had grown over the stitches. They never were dissolvable.

I was charged for the second operation, anesthesia, hospital room, and more—all due to the doctors not checking me thoroughly, and not listening to me beg to remove the stitches. Finally, they agreed not to charge me for their mistakes.

They sent me to therapy, but it's hard to learn to walk with only one leg! For months I experienced one medical mistake after another.

To brighten my day my daughter took off work to come to the nursing home to celebrate my birthday. She brought me a yummy cheesecake, some jewelry, and popcorn. Nicest B-day ever.

My Suggestions:

Keep a journal, or have someone else do it, and record every name, doctor, conversation, pill, and date. And make sure someone can speak up to the nurses and doctors for your basic needs. Have someone wash your hair and brush your teeth.

Trust your gut. I knew my stitches were infected even though they said they weren't. The infection caused me to have another surgery.

My artificial legs don't work well, but they're all I can afford. The ankles don't bend, and my pants constantly get caught in the artificial knees. With every step it's pull up, pull out, and I can't put on a belt with one hand.

Most of all an artificial leg is not a luxury, but a necessity! Congress has to pass the federal Prosthetic and Customized Orthotic Parity Act, which is intended to ensure that insurance companies across the nation provide fair and consistent coverage for these devices. They should not have annual or lifetime low insurance caps.

Having someone be there for you when you're helpless is a great blessing.

–Paula Sears

"Never underestimate your problem or your ability to deal with it."
- Robert H. Schuller

Adopt a Granny and Send Flowers, Too!

Being in the Southern California real estate business, I met a widow in her eighties who needed to sell her home.

We gave her weekly updates either by telephone or in person. I knew she was lonely in a retirement home, and had few visitors.

We'd bring coffee, a few doughnuts, and our open ears while she'd share stories of her life. It was obvious she just wanted someone to listen and feel like she still mattered. We learned she had had a very full life.

After the transaction closed we delivered a vase of flowers, along with her closing documents and the check. "Oh my goodness!" she exclaimed tearfully. "It's been 'years' since I've received flowers!" We all sat chatting for an hour. She barely took her eyes off of the vase.

I'd occasionally drop a "Thinking of You" card in

the mail. When one got returned, I knew she was gone.

I always felt bad I hadn't made more of an effort to see her, but I hoped our time together made her feel like she still mattered . . . because she did.

–Lawrence D. Elliott,
Author

Give Unconditional Love

Leon was born with a rare degenerative neuromuscular disease, which kept him weak from an early age.

One day while the family was on holiday in Spain, Leon got hit by a car and ended up with a traumatic brain injury, which made him mentally impaired and wheelchair bound for the rest of his life.

The accident should have kept him in intensive care for years, but he eventually went home on a ventilator with a tracheotomy because his parents put their life on hold for Leon.

For about five years after the accident, Leon's parents dealt with many setbacks and readmissions to intensive care. They were determined to keep Leon out of ICU, as his spirit faded in the sterile clinical environment.

Leon was a happy guy and easily entertained. He always smiled— even when he didn't feel that great. He was well loved in the community where he lived, due to his friendly and positive nature. Leon was around 20 years of age at the time, but was the size of a 5 year-old and had the mental capacity of an 8 year-old.

Leon passed away in his own home with his parents and brother at his side. Despite his limitations, major challenges and setbacks, he was blessed to have parent who loved him unconditionally. Leon lived his short life to the fullest.

– Patrik Hutzel,
Intensive Care Nurse

Ask for Grace

One night my mother called me to say my father was experiencing a stroke. I told her to go to the emergency room, have him hydrated, and I would be there as soon as I was able.

I live two hours away, so I jumped in the car and drove to Santa Ynez. On the way, I called a few of my friends and asked them to start praying for him. I also prayed the whole way there.

I knew he had a court case scheduled for the next day that was causing him stress, so I prayed to the Infinite Light to lift the burden off him, and asked that he be filled with grace. I prayed that he could forgive all people, that all people could forgive him, and that our whole family could return to peace.

The moon was shining on the black ocean and stars filled the sky. I was aware of the silence of the vast night and that I was involved in a great mystery.

When I arrived at the hospital, dad was looking

yellow and frail, not at all like himself. I sat beside him and continued to pray. Just before dawn when the hospital was very quiet, I began to feel the presence of angels. I did not see anything specifically, but a holy presence filled the room. I watched with amazement as the muscles in his face returned to normal, and I realized my father was back with me again.

He looked at me and said, "I've been healed haven't I?"

"Yes," I whispered, "I believe you have had some grace."

As the sun rose we drove back to his ranch looking at the marvelous colors of the dawn, and listening to the chorus of birds.

"Dad, this is what's important," I said. "It's loving one another that counts."

"I believe you're right," he said. He took my hand and gave it a squeeze. "I'm grateful to be alive."

–Ayn Cates Sullivan,
Author

Give Appreciation

"Some days there won't be a song in your heart. Sing anyway."
— Emory Austin

Binky was about four years old. With spindly limbs and a swollen belly, he looked like the Kermit the Frog doll. He had Prune Belly Syndrome. Born without abdominal muscles, his belly was as wrinkled as a dried prune.

Binky also had only one kidney and no bladder. His diaper was placed near his belly button, because that was where the urine dribbled out, one drop at a time.

Despite all the added work Binky created, he was an absolute joy to care for. Just coming up to his bed would make me feel better.

I remember when the order came to remove the NG (nasogastric, meaning nose-to-stomach) tube we'd been using to feed him formula. The tube is soft and doesn't hurt when in place; but going down and coming up, it creates a choking sensation as the tip passes through the lower throat. I was trying to be careful with that when he expressed concern for me. In spite of all he was going through, he was more worried about my feelings than his own. That was Binky—a most incredible kid.

The nursing staff doted on this wonderful little guy and, given the severity of his sickness, quite a few staff members got to know him.

His dying was a long, downward spiral. His one kidney began to fail. Dialysis was impossible for anyone as frail as he, and every effort to adjust his diet came to naught.

The night he died, one of the evening aides—on her own initiative—stayed with him, holding his hand until his family arrived.

After his death, twenty-four nurses and aides came to honor Binky.

Why were so many people willing to give something extra to care for Binky?

Sick and frail, Binky had nothing of material value to give us. It was the little things he did, particularly the appreciation he showed for what we did for him.

When I did something, he'd thank me, even when he was so weak, he could barely gasp out the words. You cared about him because he cared about you.

That's the magic tip I'm offering you. When you're in a hospital and feeling overwhelmed, take a moment to say something kind to those caring for you. If a nurse reaches over and adjusts your pillow, show your appreciation. If those caring for you seemed stressed outsay something like, "I can tell you're busy today. Thanks for helping me."

Remember, you're stuck in that bed with nothing else to do. You might as well be kind and thoughtful. It beats being crabby and critical.

Whether you're sick, or are there for someone who's sick, remember to show you care about the people who care, and they'll make a special effort to look out for the person who's sick.

–Mike Perry,
Author

Give Acts of Kindness - Where There's a Will There's a Way

I'm a sole practitioner lawyer who practices in the areas of wills and estate planning, and family law.

In 2008, my father was diagnosed with a brain tumor, and passed away two short months later. I was devastated. My father and I were very close, and I had difficulty coping with the loss.

The first year was the hardest, with all the milestones and important holidays to endure without him.

On December 23, 2008 my assistant came to me and said she had a will that had to be done for a very sick man. I told her I would draft the will and see the gentleman the week after Christmas. She looked at me and said, "This can't wait."

She was uncomfortable even approaching me

with this, knowing it was the first Christmas after the loss of my father. For many years she had accompanied me on emergency visits to homes and hospitals for will signings, and she knew how emotionally draining these visits were, even at the best of times.

I knew there were no other lawyers in town who would make this visit on Christmas Eve, so I drafted the will that night and went to the man's residence the following day, Christmas Eve.

The man was wheelchair bound and unable to speak. He was dying of Lou Gehrig's disease and did not seem like he had much time left. I read the will to him, and he acknowledged his approval through blinking.

I sat at the kitchen table with his wife as she signed the document on his behalf. She then told me the story of their romance. I held her hand, as she recounted how she did not know how to go on without him.

We both cried. As I packed up the documents in my briefcase, she pulled out her checkbook. I put my hand on hers and told her to put it away and let this be my gift to her.

Five months later a lovely woman walked into my office. I welcomed her and I asked how I could help. She said I already had. "You don't remember me?" she asked.

I meet hundreds of people, and couldn't place her face. She said I came to her home on Christmas Eve. I did not recognize her because she was not the tired, grieving, devastated woman I remembered from five months prior. She looked beautiful, calm and content. She said that the kindness she received from a stranger on Christmas Eve (from a lawyer no less!) was unprecedented, and helped her to move on with her life after the passing of her husband.

That short visit was the most rewarding payment I had ever received for any work I have done.

–Suzanne B. Quinn

25 Year-Old Widow: "Do What You Can."

My husband was first admitted to the hospital with liver problems. I sat by his side taking care of him in every way I could: keeping track of doctors visits and medications, administering several shots to him a day, trying to be strong for him in every discouraging moment, cooking his specialized diet, and the list is almost endless. I poured out all I had to keep him feeling comfortable, encouraged, and loved.

After seven months in and out of three different hospitals, he passed away on his 28th birthday from multi-organ failure. I was left a widow at 25 years old.

Ever since, my heart has remained with patients and their families who face hospital stays. As someone who walked through the tremendous ups and downs that patients and their caregivers face, I empathize deeply, and it's my passion to do all I can to help them.

I began by volunteering on my church's Hospital Team visiting members in the hospital. I brought them anything they needed, whether it was a meal, an encouraging book, or money to buy necessities.

I took one family under my wing. A couple's one-year-old daughter was diagnosed with cancer on her liver. She was originally told she had only a 50% chance to live.

This began a long road, and the family needed far more than a one-time visit. I often went to the hospital to talk and pray with them.

They found a doctor out of state that could perform a liver transplant for her. My bible study group came together to provide an airline ticket and money for food and hotel once they got to the hospital.

I did all I could to be a friend and would sometimes talk for hours.

Today this little girl is three years old. She's doing remarkably well after her transplant. It's now been my desire to help people by sharing my heart with them.

–Jessica Mast,
Author

Give Small "Gifts" and Keep Them Connected

At 95, my step dad (until then a very active, 'young' sharp man) was hospitalized for several months.

His greatest issue was LONELINESS.

Lots of hospital personnel came and went daily, and at first many friends and family visited. But as time wore on, the visits (and their duration) lessened.

He simply needed some company. I began to visit almost daily. I would bring a small "gift"—a news clipping, flowers from a field or garden, silly cards, or simply photos or a story about family or friends.

I realized how important it is to help people keep their connections. Often I would simply sit for 20 minutes to an hour or more; sometimes chatting, sometimes hearing his concerns, sometimes advocating for him with the plethora of medical personnel busily coming in and out, and sometimes just plain sitting and 'being' with him—a friendly and familiar face amongst all that sterility.

I always arrived and departed with hugs, and held his hand when I could.

He passed away a year ago, but we each received a wonderful gift. We both felt good for the connection. There isn't a day I don't think of him with great gratitude that I got to really know him.

I only hope this story encourages others to make an effort. I know many people dislike hospitals and feel put out to visit, but I hope this will help them realize that the simple (selfless) gesture of visiting can be a priceless gift for someone confined in a hospital, nursing or rehab facility, or simply shut in at home.

– Grace Dunklee Cohen

"After two days in the hospital,
I took a turn for the nurse.

—W.C. Fields

The Loving Side of Technology

"Technology is anything that wasn't around when you were born."

—Alan Kay

Raise Funds for Medical Bills With GiveForward.com

Insurance may not cover all the patient's needed medical expenses. That can put a huge strain on the family, and also the patient may not get needed help.

GiveForward.com provides personalized online fundraising pages to help with medical bills, and is one of the easiest ways to support a loved one in need. Their site is easy, free, and secure, and can impact a loved one's world in many ways, and help prevent a lifetime of debt.

GiveForward has raised over 60 million dollars toward medical expenses for those in need.

Here's how it works:

You set up a web page (no tech knowledge needed) on the GiveForward website. You simply answer questions, write about their situation, and list exactly what's needed—and why. You can also easily add photos and video.

For example, Paula Sears whose legs and fingers were amputated (story in this book), could barely afford the cheapest prostheses because her insurance pays only $10,000 for the total of all prostheses–FOR LIFE–regardless of how many are needed. Her friends and family created a site at GiveForward.Com to help her with her bills. See site at: http://gfwd.at/1ebaTsv

Sites to Keep Everyone Connected

"One of the nicest and most thoughtful thing people did for us was develop and update a Caring Bridge web page for us."

—Laura Ellison Cook

About Caring Bridge
(http://www.caringbridge.org)

Think of CaringBridge as an online space where you can connect, share news, and receive support. It's your very own health social network, coming together on your personalized website. And thanks to those who donate, Caring Bridge is available 24/7 to anyone, anywhere, at no cost.

CaringBridge Offers:

- CaringBridge Sites

  Personal, protected web sites make it easy to stay connected during any type of health event. Family and friends can visit the site to stay informed and leave supportive messages.

- Support Planner

  Their SupportPlanner is a calendar that helps family and friends coordinate care and organize helpful tasks, like bringing a meal, offering rides, taking care of pets, and other needs.

And It's Easy

It takes just minutes to start a Site, set up a Support Planner, or join someone's community.

Over a half a million people connect through CaringBridge each day, amplifying love, hope and compassion.

That's a lot of love.

Another Helpful Site: FamilyeJournal

One of the greatest ways to help people who are sick and burdened with extended stays in a hospital is to maintain a connection with them.

It can be difficult for large groups, or far-away family/friends to visit a sick loved-one, but there's still a great way to connect, on a deeper level, if the patient is able to read or write.

Families can stay connected by using a simple website called Familyejournal.com. This website uses a Q&A format to connect family members in a fun and meaningful way. Anyone 8+ can answer the questions and read answers from family members and the hospital patient.

The website is free, private, and creates a level of closeness that is powerful and healing.

–Kevin Strauss

Organize Meals with Free Service

In December of 2007, a close friend of ours collapsed from the sudden onset of a heart condition.

The phone rang day and night because family, friends, and neighbors wanted to help by bringing meals to her husband and four young children. We felt overwhelmed by the task of coordinating meals, but we wanted to help and knew the meals were needed.

As a result, we designed a site that eliminated the need for making and receiving time-consuming phone calls.

Once the site was finished, we realized that meal scheduling is done not just when tragedy strikes, but when babies are born, when friends are receiving medical treatments, and in so many other situations.

Before we knew it, many of our friends were making use of TakeThemAMeal.com and word was spreading. Just recently, a child in our community was severely injured. The family posted a link to their TakeThemAMeal.com account on their blog, and a meal schedule for several months was filled overnight.

We made TakeThemAMeal.com to help one family we care about deeply, which made the site worthwhile. Now we'd like to share this tool, so others may be helped as well.

Feel free to use it often, and tell your family, friends and co-workers about it. It's absolutely free!

See ideas from the pros on recipes and transport tips:
http://bit.ly/1cjBthr

They have a schedule that's so easy to fill out and keep everyone informed.

—*Adina Bailey,*
Founder, COO

Video Chat

My mother-in-law has terminal cancer. Her sense of humor is truly inspiring in the face of what she is going through. A lot of our communication with her has been through Facetime (a free video application on the Macintosh computers. It's like Skype, a video chat service). She lives in UK and we're in Sydney. It's a great way for us to visit with her when we're so many miles apart.

You can sign up for video chats on Skype.com. It's easy to do, and will keep you in contact with anyone anywhere in the world—all for free!

Google Hangouts is another free video chat service that brings conversations to life with photos, emoji, and even enables both one-on-one chats and group chats with up to ten people at a time. It connects across computers, Android and Apple devices. Here's a video of how Google hangouts works: http://bit.ly/HAjW6z

–Helen Ashley

Show Movies in Their Room

Watch TV shows and movies anytime, anywhere with Netflix.

It can be ordered for laptops, iPads, and mobile devices too.

Sick people will have a more enjoyable stay when they can watch what they want, when they want, rather than waiting for their favorite shows, or just watching whatever is on.

Sign up at: https://signup.netflix.com/

Netflix recurring membership is $7.99 a month, includes a one-month free offer. Simply cancel anytime during your one-month free membership, and you will not be charged.

Also, many facilities have DVD players, or bring yours and hook it up.

Or you can rent videos from Redbox, which has over 36,000 locations. Find your location here:

http://www.redbox.com/locations

Redbox.com can even stream videos anywhere, anytime. They too have a free one-month trial membership.

You can check out videos from the library. Most are free. Some libraries may charge around $1 for a week or two.

–Edna Ma,
MD, board certified anesthesiologist

Play Video Games

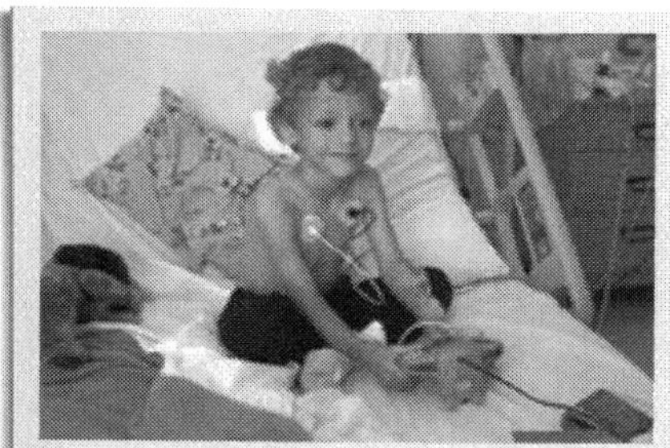

A sick child plays Mario Kart 64 in a hospital in New Mexico. This was made possible by get well gamers

Gone are the days when a child would be entertained by hours of television. Now they can lose themselves in games for hours. Kids LOVE playing video games!

I'm the co-chair and co-creator of a large gaming convention called Gam3rCon (http://www.gam3rcon.com/) and each year we do a folk concert (geek folk music) to benefit the nonprofit, Get Well Gamers. (http://www.getwellgamers.org/)

This group provides video game systems to kids who are stuck in the hospital.

Even if a family can't get games through GWG, I would suggest they bring a game system to the hospital. Even adults can benefit from that sort of escapism.

– *Walter Meyer,*
co-creator Gam3rCon

Awesome Thing to Do!

Donate your new or used video games, systems, controllers, and other accessories to this charity so they can be distributed to hospitals. See info in the back of this book.

Get Books, Videos, Music, and Audio Books—Online and Offline

Did you know that many of the audio and Kindle books you see on Amazon are free ONLINE on your public library's web site?

Go to your library's website, click the digital section, and search for the item you want. When you find it, simply download your selection to your device. They have books, CDs, and videos for every device.

You can also go to overdrive.com. They have the largest digital catalog available with over one million digital titles. The search will tell you which libraries have the title you want.

http://search.overdrive.com/

When the digital item expires, usually in about three weeks, it simply disappears. No more late fees. No more returns.

It also eliminates clutter since it's all on a device.

By the way, you can go to the library and check out the physical books, audio books, and videos. Some patients don't have the energy to read holding a book, so audio books and videos are a great idea.

And did you know that most libraries also have delivery services for home bound and hospitalized people. They'll deliver books and audios right to their doors!

–Ruth Wilkes,
Children's book author, editor

Create Video Greeting Cards

A dear friend, who lives in New Jersey, had been experiencing health issues for quite some time. To comfort her, I sent her a video greeting card. I live in Los Angeles, so the goal was to make her smile and let her know I was there in spirit. The video was 2.5 minutes of music, personal pictures, and voice-overs by me wishing her well.

Here's my uplifting video I made for my friend:

http://youtu.be/Z1tnNkCfUJg

–Yolonda Brinkley,
Marketing and PR Strategist

Another Video To Cheer Them Up

After my mother's open-heart surgery our family started spending Christmas at different places (Vegas, London, Williamsburg), or anywhere that offered a unique and enjoyable memory with mom.

We decided to take little Katy, my oldest brother's daughter, to Disneyland. Unfortunately, mom wasn't feeling well enough for the trip. So I video taped the adventure, and had my friend Todd Warren Howard, an independent filmmaker, edit the footage.

When he finally finished the project, complete with sound effects and humorous voice-overs—mom was delighted!

"It was like going to Disneyland," she said, "without dealing with the crowds."

She passed away a few months later, but at least she enjoyed her final Christmas at Disneyland with little Katy.

–David Andrew Lloyd,
Screenwriter

Have Them Hear Everyone's Love

This is something they'll always remember and cherish!

Ask all the sick person's friends to call this free service, SimpleVoiceBox.com, and leave a message saying what they love about the person, and add their get well wishes.

You can contact everyone the patient knows by email, Twitter, or private message people from their Facebook page.

SimpleVoiceBox.com works like this. When you sign up on their site you're given a phone number and access code.

You give everyone this number and code to call. Once they call they enter in the access number and leave their message, just like on an answering machine.

You simply download all the messages and

email them to the person who's ill, or upload them to an mp3 player, or burn to CD.

Make sure you ask people to give fun and/or heart-warming messages saying what they love about the person.

The sick person will be deeply touched to hear and feel everyone's love and kindness.

Give Them Their Own Radio Station

The patient's favorite music can lift their spirits and calm or enliven the room.

There's a free service called Pandora that will play music on your mobile device (Nook, Kindle fire, iPad, iPod, iPhone, Blackberry, Android, Windows Phone, and on PC or Mac computers).

http://www.pandora.com/everywhere/mobile

You can create the patient's own music stations with their favorite artists on each station.

So let's say they like Frank Sinatra. You can have an entire channel play Frank's songs.

Or, some hospitals and rehabs have music channels on TV, so patients can listen to all types of commercial-free music from soothing jazz to rock and roll. Ask the staff to help you find the station.

Show 'Em the Best of YouTube

YouTube has some of the most heart-warming, inspirational, funny, and amazing videos that can really lift one's mood.

These are popular ones. You may have seen some, but it's fun to see these excellent videos again!

Here are a few examples:

Motivational

Don't ever give up. The body can heal.
http://bit.ly/KoX3hi

No arms. No legs. No worries.
http://bit.ly/aT3a99

Heart Warming

A homeless boy enters singing contest.
http://bit.ly/joA7i0

Free hugs
http://bit.ly/GaEj

Fun

The wedding dance.
http://bit.ly/Z7vMw

The biggest hug ever.
http://bit.ly/rdcgkK

Old man dancing to Zeplin.
http://bit.ly/19b9ph

Animals

Laugh out loud funny. Dog dances to rap music.
http://bit.ly/Yyp55q

Adorable! Guy sings puppies to sleep.
http://bit.ly/aoGaLR

Always keep hope. Dog breaks his back, but ends up running again.
http://bit.ly/16dGvUd

Dog playing the piano.
http://bit.ly/gq6PdX

Amazing Dog Skidboot will touch your heart.
http://bit.ly/lNdpsS

Dog nods head to guitar music.
http://bit.ly/sD50vL

Yoga time with cute dog.
http://bit.ly/1bgBr6v

Snuggle with a seal.
http://bit.ly/wW8JGD

Singers and Dancers

Guy at gas station sings and has fun, but doesn't know he's on the Jay Leno show.
http://bit.ly/132KxxA

13 Year-Old Sings.
http://bit.ly/Sjbuar

Josh Groban sings, *You Are Love-Don't Give Up*!
http://bit.ly/16wpAo

Two-year-old dances to Elvis.
http://bit.ly/H6UeFZ

Nervous woman sings *"Funny Little Valentine."*
http://bit.ly/1dIIshJ

Boy sings to Ellen DeGeneres.
http://huff.to/11me76J

Nature

What a wonderful world. Beautiful!
http://bit.ly/uIeIIq

Nature at work.
http://bit.ly/18xecXK

Most spectacular landscapes in the world.
http://bit.ly/1enSDLt

Inspirational

Wayne Dyer - Power of Intention.
http://bit.ly/1f4yfOj

Jessica's affirmations.
http://bit.ly/4JqwE6

Steve Jobs on failure.
http://bit.ly/w0FvoO

86 year-old gymnast.
http://bit.ly/12bL0ke

If You Really Knew Me. High school students relate to each other.
http://on.mtv.com/9qNYQq

An audio reading of the book, *The Magic of Believing*. Comedian Phyllis Diller attributes all her success to this book.
http://bit.ly/1dnPGHN

Informative

Sitting kills.
http://bit.ly/1bDT5PS

Video Summaries of Popular Books.
http://bit.ly/1a2Na7R

Set Up An Amazon Wish List

My adult daughter was recently hospitalized due to a stroke, and is now going through Rehab at home.

Her friends set up an Amazon Wish List (it's kind of like a bridal registry) for her, which included pajamas, fruit basket and gift cards, so those who wanted to do something for her could send her what she wanted or needed.

They called me and asked me for ideas. Then, through social media, they spread the word and shared the link. Great idea!

–Janet Miserandino

Watch New, Fun Ways to Learn

TED.com brings together the world's most fascinating thinkers and doers who are challenged to give the talk of their lives (in 18 minutes or less). These free presentations are enjoyed by millions of people at Ted.com.

Most places have WI-FI you can log on to the Internet with your computer, phone, eReaders, or podcasts. Simply go to TED talks at:

www.Ted.com

More than 1500 TED Talks are now available, with more added each week.

Udemy.com is a site that offers thousands of online free and pay courses.

You can learn every type of topic: Technology,

business, design, arts, photography, health, fitness, lifestyle, math, science, education, languages, music, crafts, hobbies, sports, games, and more.

Another site is SkillShare.com, which also has excellent video courses for around $9.95 a month, and you can cancel anytime.

With both sites, you receive courses instantly and go at your own pace.

Also get inspired watching free TED.com presentations. TED brings together the world's most fascinating thinkers and doers who are challenged to give the talk of their lives (in 18 minutes or less).

–Judy Gibbons,
Realtor

Ways to Stay in Touch

Be Consistent

After major surgery my sister, who lived in another state, called me in my room at the same time every night to say, "Good Night and hope you feel a little better!"

It meant the world to me! It was the highlight of my day and something I really looked forward to!

–Mary Sullivan,
Author

Emailing

It's important to give a list of phone numbers and email addresses to let the sick friend know that they can always call or email when they want to connect with others.

–Lorraine Milton,
Author

Text Messages

As a CHD patient and TP survivor, my best advice for patients are fun visits, phone calls, or better yet, text messages.

From the moment you're alone in the hospital you're lonely. No matter how high-spirited you are and how great the nursing staff is, the tendency for depression in patients grows every day they remain in the hospital.

There's healing in humor, so give books with humor.

To promote emotional healing, train yourself to live in gratitude. Share the gift of you with the world, and cherish each new day that brings you the opportunity to look into the eyes of those you love.

–Lorelei Hill
Transplant/Congenital Advisor

"You have power over your mind –
not outside events.
Realize this, and you will find strength."

— Marcus Aurelius

Awesome Ideas for Health Advocates, Care Partners and Caregivers

"The most important exercise any of us will ever do is reaching out and lifting someone else up."
— Bill Phillips

Have Eyes Wide Open

I certainly wasn't prepared for the series of medical errors that struck my family.

After a successful lung transplant at a top academic medical center, my father died from complications resulting from a fall that went untreated for 57 hours, which led to pneumonia, blood clots, a pulmonary embolism, MRSA and C diff.

My husband spent 18 months recovering from sepsis and a VRE infection, stemming from improper surgery preparation and care afterward. My young son would have undergone an unnecessary operation had I not questioned a doctor and sought a second opinion.

Determined to help other families avoid similar fates, I slogged through nursing textbooks, talked to medical and patient safety experts, searched through healthcare studies and more.

As a result, I compiled my research into *Safe & Sound in the Hospital,* a new handbook designed to provide a series of practical tips, creative tools, and quick checklists that care partners can use to help prevent common hospital hazards and promote a safe recovery.

This guide is my way of transforming my family's tragedies into better outcomes for others. Tips include:

• **Keep your loved one safe from infection.**
Make sure everyone—especially doctors and nurses—washes his or her hands before touching your loved one. Make colorful tent card signs for your loved one's room with messages like "Thank you for washing your hands!" Or, "For my safety, please wash your hands." (The *Wall Street Journal* reports only 50% of doctors and staff comply with hand- washing hygiene. "**Infections picked up in hospitals, nursing homes and doctor's offices affect more than 1 million patients and are linked to nearly 100,000 deaths a year.**" http://on.wsj.com/19d8drg)

• **Keep Handy Wipes Handy**
Clean TV remotes, door knobs, telephones, bed rails, call buttons, faucets, toilet flush levers and

personal items with alcohol wipes *and* bleach wipes to help zap Superbugs and C. diff spores. Repeat cleaning after every touch or brush with clothing—doctors' jackets and scrubs and nurses' uniforms are like Trojan Horses, carrying bugs all over the hospital.

• **Find out how to call for a Rapid Response Team**
Trust your gut. Call if you feel like your loved one is going downhill and no one seems to be taking action.

• **If possible, schedule surgeries mid-week and avoid holiday times.**
If complications arise you'll want to be able to reach your doctor and the "A" team.

• **Ask the nurse to pause and double-check each medication just before it's given.**
Verify the prescription, the dose *and* intended patient. NEVER interrupt a nurse in the middle of administering a drug unless you sense a mistake. Nurses have accidentally mixed up meds, so always double-check meds.

• **Virtually every patient is at risk to take a fall.**
Look for items in the room that might cause a fall, and bring non-skid socks or slippers for them to wear. Also, ask the nurses about a cane for your loved one to use.

Make sure someone is available to help your loved one to the bathroom and back. Have rehab or health specialists demonstrate to older people how to fall if they start falling. This prepares them so if they ever do fall, they can fall in a safer way.

One in three patients is accidentally harmed in U.S. hospitals every year, according to a 2011 study from *Health Affairs*, a health policy journal. But these tips can help fill the cracks in hospital care.

We need more eyes and ears on patients, and who could be more patient-centered care partners than families?

It's so important for families to be engaged, vigilant, and keep their eyes wide open when someone they love is in the hospital.

–Karen Curtis,
Author

Top Ten List of Caring

When my father-in-law was dying, he asked my husband and me if we would move in to care for my mother-in-law.

She was very ill, and needed a lot of care. But she was angry and felt she was losing her independence.

I knew the best medicine for any ailments was laughter. I asked her about what movies and music she liked. She shared that she loved Bob Hope, Big Band Music, and a television show, *Jack Benny.* So I bought all the collections of Bob Hope, *Jack Benny,* and Big Band Music. She'd laugh so much and forget about her aches and pains.

We became very close during the ten years that I was her main caregiver. She became very loving and kind.

She felt much better from the meditation and exercises I taught her. She loved to meditate, which she had never learned before. She said it helped her to relax and not be in so much pain.

She shared with me her dreams of taking a cruise to Alaska. I taught her how to use positive thinking and creative visualization, which is using your imagination to create outcomes you desire.

She did it, and ended up taking an amazing cruise to Alaska with her youngest daughter. She told me it was a dream come true.

Here are some of the suggestions I would offer to anyone who is a caregiver for someone who is sick.

10. Bring him or her their favorites, whether it is in music, videos, or food.

9. Appreciate that you have another precious day to be with them.

8. Have patience, and do your best to be completely present with them.

7. Share positive thinking. Help your loved one realize positive thinking can affect their health and empower them.

6. Have lots of compassion, and think of how you would want to be treated.

5. Teach your loved one how to take care of themselves, and try to give them easy

tasks to build their confidence. It's very difficult for people to be dependent on someone.

4. Do things that make you happy, and you'll be enjoying the precious time you have with your loved one. Remember that everything is transitory, and cherish every moment knowing you're always making memories.

3. Learn to be still and connect with your inner guidance. Spend time re-charging your battery every day.

2. Find a way to have fun while you are caring for a sick person. Your energy is contagious, and if you are cheerful you can really raise the positive energy level in a room.

1. Make sure to take care of yourself and make time to give self-care. If your well is dry you can't give anyone a drink.

–Karen Palmer,
Founder and CEO of Eco Angels

Sit in Compassion

Often when being with a person who is very ill or in pain, it seems most natural to feel sorry for the person, or to feel an urgent need to fix or help them. *When help is not needed,* negative feelings don't do the sick person any good, or serve you in any way.

Compassion is "being" with someone where they are. It doesn't mean to take the sorrow or suffering on to you, or be in worry or distress, but instead to be present with a state of understanding.

Sitting in compassion with someone enhances intimacy between you and the person who is sick, or in pain. It helps them to feel heard, and it's easier to speak.

This meeting of the minds and hearts often brings much peace to both parties. The synergy can bring on a level of acceptance, which is a vital part of life.

–Susan "Chef Teton" Campbell,
Chef and Nutrition Educator

Be of Contribution

"Life's challenges are not supposed to paralyze you; they're supposed to help you discover who you are."
— Bernice Johnson Reagon

A friend had shoulder surgery, and was very limited in what she could do. I moved into her spare bedroom. For ten days I cooked, cleaned, and chauffeured her. I was on call 24/7 and catered to her every need. It was great to be able to help her so much.

As I reflect more on the situation, I felt a kind of freedom in just totally being there for another human being. I learned a lot about myself in terms of how patient, caring, and selfless I could be. No thinking about anything other than how can I help this person was very freeing.

Besides a sense of freedom, I also felt a sense of calm rising above all the mundane aspects of everyday living. It became almost like a spiritual bliss to be so committed to someone else's well-being.

Fortunately, it lasted 10 days over the holidays, and I was able to get back to taking care of myself.

I donate my time giving workshops for teens, the unemployed, and the homeless, which gives me some of the same positive feelings.

Being of contribution to others is one of the best things we can do for ourselves.

–Ronald Kaufman,
Seminar Leader/Executive Coach/Author

Organize and Make Copies of Medical Information

Patients often have to see many doctors, rehab specialists, nurses, insurance representatives, and other health care professionals.

They all ask the same questions:
"When was the surgery?"
"What did they operate on?"
"What medications are you on, and what dosage?"
"What is the level of your pain?"

Writing everything down actually saves time (you're not repeating the same answers) and is more accurate because you can make copies to give to all the health care people who need the information.

1) Make one page listing all their medications (this is also great for the patient to keep track of his or her meds).

   It's important that the lists are typed to

help avoid errors. There have been mix-ups because some medications have similar names, or the dosage was misread.

a) List the meds, their colors and shapes.

b) List the amounts.

c) Write the times when the meds are to be taken.

d) The purpose of the meds.

e) How long the patient has been on that med—the date when they started taking the med. (*That's important because of side effects. For example, if they suddenly get extremely weak and tired around the time they started taking a new drug, it could be just a side effect of the drug.)*

2) Make a copy of their driver's license and insurance cards on another page.

3) List the dates of surgeries, and what exactly was done.

4) Write the symptoms the patient is having now, and what's being done.

5) Include all the doctors' names and phone numbers, and who to contact if there's an emergency.

Then make copies to hand out to everyone involved.

It may sound like a lot to do, but you're only doing it once and making copies. It saves everyone asking the same questions, and it'll be more accurate.

My husband and I have personally experienced a pharmacist putting the wrong labels on our meds. My husband's prescription had my name on the label, and my prescription had his name. Since I knew the color and shape of my meds, I caught the error right away. Knowing this avoided what could have been a disaster.

Here's a template for an example of an easy-to-follow list of medications for a patient who's at home, but is on a lot of meds. To eliminate mistakes it shows when to take the meds, the amounts, what they are for, the color and shape of the pills, and the phone numbers of doctors and emergency contacts.

Remember, there are potential risks from combining various medications. Errors made dispensing drugs are not uncommon. ALWAYS discuss all discrepancies or concerns with their doctors.

–Mary Hanson,
Nurse

SAMPLE SHEET FOR MEDICATIONS	
BEFORE BREAKFAST	1 **LEVOTHYROXINE** (0.025 mg) **Thyroid**-round-peach 1 **FINASTERIDE** (5mg) **prostate** blue-oval
AT BREAKFAST	1 **CARVEDILOL** (3.125 mg) **Blood pressure**-tiny-white-oval, **1st one** (TWICE DAILY) 1 **OMEPRAZOLE** (20mg) **stomach**-white-oval 1 **SOTALOL** (80mg) **heart**-blue-oval **1st one** (TWICE DAILY) 1 **FUROSIMIDE** (40 mg) **swelling ankles**-round-white **1st one** (TWICE DAILY) 1 **LISINOPRIL** (5mg) **high blood pressure**-round-pin 1 **CALCIUM CITRATE CAPS--- 1st one** white (TWICE DAILY) 1 **FERROUS SULFATE** (325mg) **iron** red
AT DINNER (EVE)	1 **LIPITOR** (20mg) **cholesterol**-peach-oval 1 **CLOPIDOGREL BISULFATE** (75mg) **blood thinner** round-pink 1 **ASPIRIN** (325mg) white 1 **SOTALOL** (80mg) **heart**-oval-blue (**2nd one**) **1 CARVEDILOL blood pressure** tiny-white-oval **2nd one** 1 **FUROSIMIDE** (40 mg) **swelling ankles**-round-white **2nd one** 1 **CHOLECALCIFEROL** (1000 Units) **Vitamin D** soft gel 1 **SIMVASTATIN** (20 mg) **cholesterol** peach oval 1 **SOTALOL HCl (AF)** (80 mg) **heart** blue-oval **2nd one** **1 CYANOCOBALAMIN** vitamin B (1000 MCG/ML) **1 shot/month**

Add the names and phone numbers of all doctors and emergency contact phone numbers at the bottom.

Baby Monitor for Adults

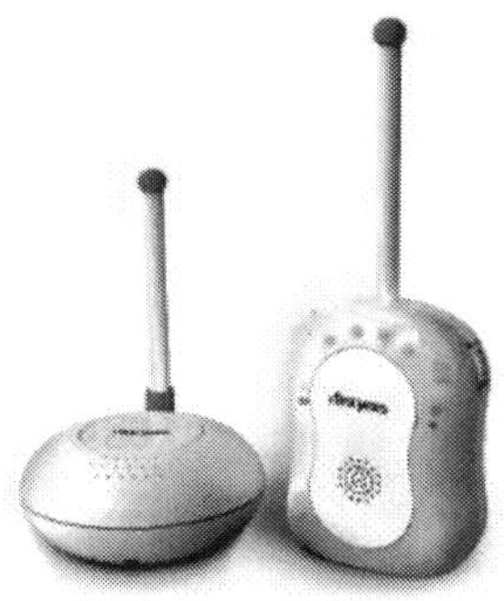

If a patient is recuperating in another part of the house you can use a baby monitor. You can hear them from anywhere in, or just outside the house, so you will know when they want something.

The baby monitor has a belt clip, so it's easy to carry with you. It can also come with two receivers, so you can put them in different rooms of the house, or give one to another caregiver.

Crisp and Clear by First Years is a good baby monitor (pictured here). It's around $30 at Target or Amazon.

Being There

Dad was in the hospital for nearly eight months straight. He had three major surgeries, a bleed to the brain, and many other smaller operations. He had tubes coming out of his nose for six months, and tubes out of his sides for seven. He lost more than1/3 of his body weight.

He rarely complained and was always so happy that we were with him the entire time.

He endured pain and discomfort, cold and wet, noise, and bright lights. He wrestled with the perceived humiliation of others caring for his private bodily functions, and answered the same questions from different registrars, specialists and general medical staff over and over again. At all times he was kind and gentle, and grateful for the staff that cared for him. He did his absolute best.

I didn't give a second thought to dedicating six days a week to visiting dad at that time; there was no other place I wanted to be.

Many days I'd just sit with him, sometimes saying nothing at all, or we listened to his favorite music.

Other times I'd bring 'real' food for him, which he could occasionally enjoy. Sometimes we'd take a walk when he had the strength . . . other times we'd talk about walks he did in his life. We'd reminisce about his beloved Qantas Airways. He was an engineer there.

Mostly his last seven months were happy. I have many fond memories of creating a room that felt more like home; of taking dad into the garden, which he loved so much; of rubbing his sore and aching back, and rubbing cream on his drying and fragile skin.

My last hours with dad were spent watching him as his breathing labored.

My final opportunity to help him was to read from a beautiful book on Aviation History. I started reading because dad's coughing was getting worse and worse. Quite frankly, I was sitting in the chair wiping tears from my eyes watching him in so much discomfort.

It seemed soothing for him to listen to the stories of The Wright Brothers, and other great aviators . . . and eventually, the more he listened, the less he thought about his discomfort, and he was able to stop coughing completely.

Dad passed the next day just before I could get to him. He passed on my daughter's 18th birthday; they were always very close, and now will be tied together in this special way.

The journey with dad, until his passing some 22 months after he first became ill, was the most treasured time in my life.

–Lisa Gorman

Awesome Thing to Do!

Do They Need to Wear a Medical Alert Button?

A medical alert button, worn around the neck, can be pressed to get emergency help instantly.

When getting an alert, make sure there are no hidden fees, no set-up charges, no contracts, their operators are all in the US, and they'll stay on with you till help arrives. See if you can get a locked in cost, or they'll raise the price a little every year, which soon adds up.

Phillips Lifeline is good because it monitors if they fall, and will send help.

http://www.lifelinesys.com/content/

Go With the Flow

I always had the motto that I should "go with the flow" in regard to helping the elderly.

I began care giving with a huge hesitance; a friend asked me to fill in for her as dining room manager at a high-end retirement facility.

Well, that turned into an eye opening two-year gig, full of great moments.

Every person I've helped became part of my family. At Claire's memorial, her daughter Janet, told how one day she happened to see her mom and me, I was her caregiver, crouched down in the garage sanding Claire's bumper, which we eventually spray-painted!

Don and Lucille became the parents I no longer had. For hours we'd reminisce, over horrid coffee, on cold winter mornings about them growing up on farms in Wisconsin without electricity or running water!

I not only knew their entire family by name, but

also learned of their high school courtship, Don's poverty, and the various challenges the two faced in their 60 years of marriage.

Don, a majorly successful engineer with a doctorate, mowed lawns in the neighborhood after retiring. He took special care of everyone with phenomenal kindness and a sense of responsibility for others.

With a tear, I close by telling of the last few months. Prostate cancer got my guy—it was terrible. The hospice staff brought much loving comfort to Don, something he had never allowed himself to experience. It was wonderful to see that Don, the one who took care of everyone, was finally experiencing being nurtured.

There was a sense of gratitude he exuded, which made us all smile and cry.

Lucille, his darling wife, could not muster the will to live after his passing. We, (her son, daughter, myself) tried every little thing in our power to help her want to go on, but it was only Don who knew the secret to her happiness. She was never the same, and it was a blessing when poor Lucille passed.

I do not do this work any longer.

The last heartstring was broken.

I cherish Don's old glasses from the 50's, which have my prescription in them. His son said they looked great on me and let me have them.

I'm warmed by Lucille's favorite shawl, and Claire's handmade bowl greets me every day as I walk upstairs.

The best tips I can give others on care giving would be:

Profound empathy: Growing old can be difficult—possible loss of so much freedom, and so many more physical discomforts.

Listening: The elderly enjoy reliving their past. I memorized ALL of Lucille's stories. She so enjoyed them—a broken record as it were! This is what made her happy, but after Don died, she no longer even wanted to rehash those stories — so sad.

Lastly, go with the flow: Every person I took care of was entirely different. I had to be especially flexible, but perhaps this was a good life lesson.

–Alice Mosdel

Creative Ideas from An Awesome Caregiver

Lynne Barstow is a caregiver who's constantly coming up with fun ideas to brighten her client's lives.

When one client, Harriet, was in the hospital, Lynne prepared a Caesar salad right at Harriet's bedside, complete with a glass decorative bowl and wooden servers. Harriet felt like she had been temporarily transported to a five-star restaurant.

When Lynne found out Harriet's favorite singer was Dean Martin, she purchased all Dean's CDs. Dean's smoothing voice was therapeutic since Harriet just loved hearing him croon.

Lynne looks for extra things she can do to be of service. As long as she's doing a job, she figures she might as well do a spectacular job. She's washed windows, given facials, organized closets, gone grocery shopping, prepared healthy salads, made and served special meals, walked the dog, put in extra hours, and even put together parties for her care giving clients.

Naturally, Lynne's clients look forward to her arriving since she always makes sure she arrives in a positive mood. Her clients feel better simply by being around her. So give your loved one a joy ride, and like Lynne, keep a clear intention to brighten people's lives and bring them all your happiness.

–Eva O'Neil

More Advocate Tips

In 1999, when my mom was in the hospital for cancer, she liked having me there to help make her comfortable . . . fluff pillows, massage her legs, feet, back, and fetch ice chips.

My father kept a record of what meds she was on, and how often, so we could keep track, and find nurses when she was due to have her pain meds . . . they would have to take time to go down to the dispensary and seemed to appreciate the gentle reminder :-) We didn't nag, just respectful.

Sometimes, you need that advocate, too . . . the patient doesn't want to look like they're whining or complaining.

–Lara Fabans

Check Their Meds

When I visited my mom I thought she had dementia because she seemed totally out of it, so I switched to a doctor who specializes in elderly patients. The geriatric doctor said she was just over medicated, and weaned her off many of her meds. It wasn't long before I noticed a huge positive improvement.

I know two people who had similar experiences. One friend's mother was so weak she couldn't even stand. It was the side effect of her meds. The doctor took her off some of her drugs, and she soon improved regaining her strength.

When I walk through my mom's nursing home I see many people who seem out of it. I wonder if it's because they're older, or if they're just on too many meds.

I want to let others know that over medicating can also have side effects. *Always discuss anything about their medications with their doctors. Do NOT try to control meds yourself.*

–Sandra Woodsides

Tips for Caring for Someone Elderly or Sick

Look into their eyes and be a good listener.

Give them a loving gentle touch.

Brush their hair.

Use lotion on their hands and feet.

Tell them how much they mean to you, and what you have learned from knowing them.

Have a sense of humor and make them laugh!

Talk about their lives (what they can remember of it) from childhood memories to adulthood.

Share your life with them, too. It gives them other things to think about.

If they like dogs, bring one to them to pet and love.

Bring them their favorite foods.

Google something they are interested in, and read about it.

Create a cheerful environment with flowers, sunlight, and music.

Give them kisses and hugs.

–Devon Greene,
Volunteer Caregiver

Ensure your loved one is getting the best care possible, fight for it, and be organized, ask questions, make lists, and stay positive.

And will yourself to go to sleep at night. You can't help someone if you're exhausted.

–Laura Ellison Cook

Ask for a Brain Monitor During Surgery

"The risks of being over-anesthetized are many, including delirium, long-tern dementia, memory loss, and even death."
-Dr. Barry Friedberg

Stanford trained and board certified anesthesiologist for over three decades, Barry Friedberg, MD, wrote the book, *Getting Over Going Under,* to urge people to ask for a direct brain activity monitor (costs $20) during surgery, so they can receive the correct amount of anesthesia.

Too little anesthesia could result in you waking up during surgery, but being unable to alert your anesthesiologist. Too much anesthesia could cause you to have delirium, or even irreversible dementia after your anesthesia.

Dr. Friedberg states, "Using a brain monitor will often lessen the drug dosage up to 30 percent per procedure." It will monitor the exact amount needed for the patient.

He started the private, non-profit organization called Goldilocks Anesthesia Foundation. http://goldilocksanesthesiafoundation.org/

The public education message of the Foundation is "No major surgery under anesthesia without a brain monitor."

The Friedberg Method of Goldilocks Anesthesia has a phenomenal safety record, and allows the anesthesiologist to administer the right amount of anesthesia—not too little and not too much.

Dr. Friedberg has absolutely no financial connection with brain monitor manufacturers, or anesthetic drug producers. His mission is to educate people on avoiding the risks of too much anesthesia, which can affect people mentally, and even cause death.

"Compassion doesn't say, 'What can the world do for me?' but rather, 'How can I serve the world?' It is the feeling you access when looking at the world through the eyes of the divine heart."

—Debbie Ford, Author

Yummy Food Ideas

"Food is our common ground, a universal experience."

—James Beard

Special Deliveries

From a Restaurant

To lift the spirit of a man who had done me a good turn, I once had a steak sent to his hospital room from the finest steak place. He was crazy happy about it!

–Tina Mosetis

Special Delivery from Kids

As a caregiver I had a couple clients in the hospital and in a rehab facility that needed some cheering up, so I dressed three of my toddler grandchildren ages 4, 3, and 2 in angel costumes. I gave two of them baskets full of a variety of chocolates and hard candy, including sugar free, and gave my oldest grandson red roses to carry.

After we finished our visits the two older kids asked if they could do it again since they felt the joy from patients and staff.

This activity also teaches our grandchildren to care and respect the elderly and be compassionate. My grandson liked it because he said, "I get lots of hugs!"

–Angil Tarach-Ritchey RN,
GCM, Eldercare Expert

Shake Things Up

One of our favorite things to do is to kick off the St. Patrick's Day holiday season with Shamrock Shakes. It's been an annual tradition.

The year our friend Tara was hospitalized with cancer, we decided to surprise Tara, her family, and her entire care team by showing up at the hospital with Shamrock Shakes for everyone!

It may sound strange, but it brought a sense of normalcy to her life. With what she was going through, it gave her a chance to laugh and remember when we made our own Shamrock Shakes and turned everyone's mouth green.

We tricked our friend Julie, who dared to say that McDonalds made a better shake, into a taste test where our homemade shake was victorious. Little did Julie know that we didn't have time to run out to McDonalds, so we poured our shake into two glasses and asked her to pick the best!

This past year we kept the tradition alive and revived our homemade Shamrock Shakes. What fun! The story was all about how we came to the hospital and fooled Julie.

–D. Nikki Wheeler

Send Personal Deliveries

When I moved to Florida by myself in the 70's I unexpectedly needed surgery.

My boyfriend back in Chicago (Ben Creed) felt terrible that neither one of us knew anyone in Florida!

He wrote a letter addressed to: Manager of Ft Lauderdale "Wendy's," a brand new chain restaurant at the time.

The letter included a $10 bill and explained that his girlfriend was in the hospital without friends or family, and would so love a Frosty. He added, "If you're a guy, trust me and deliver this yourself. She's worth the trip."

Fortunately, Wendy's manager had a big heart.

A surprise knock came on my hospital room door, and in walked a man in a Wendy's uniform with a cooler full of Frosty's as well as a bag of burgers and fries! "Hi, who are you?" I asked. He smiled, "Ben sent me."

We chatted as I ate my Frosty, and then he handed me the letter that Ben had mailed to him. (I still have it!)

He wished me well, and as he left said, "By the way, he was right. You were worth the trouble."

What a sweet, sweet experience!

–Janet Collins Jordan

Bring Good Cooking

As a hospice nurse, this was a common challenge. I try to find out what the patient loves, wants, and longs for in life.

One mother and daughter came in to visit grandma, who wasn't talkative, or very active.

When I spoke to them they mentioned that grandma really liked to cook. So I suggested that every night they make a special meal, bring it in, and talk about it. That did the trick.

It was nothing fancy, just good cooking. Their mom perked up.

They thanked me for making her last days memorable and joyous, celebrating what was, rather than mourning what was to come.

–Jonathan Steele,
Hospice nurse

Feed Their Family

One of the best ways that I can help someone is through a meal.

When you're sick the last thing that you need to worry about is feeding your family; it takes all the energy that you can find just to take care of yourself.

Sometimes when I am cooking, I like to make double batches of meals that freeze well. These usually include soups, lasagnas, sauces, and burritos. I can just drop these ready-to-go meals off at a friend's house.

Once I made 40 bean, beef, and cheese burritos for the freezer. I had a friend that could use some cheering up, so I made some Mexican rice and took ten burritos to their home.

Another time I took two different kinds of freezer chili to a friend that was sick. She had four teenagers at home, and was so thankful that she didn't have to worry about feeding her family. She was able to rest, save her energy, and take care of herself.

–Karen Weideman,
Teacher, blogger

Bring Care Baskets to the Waiting Room

I take gift baskets to friends whose family members are in the intensive care unit. The friends are under a lot of stress, and spend many hours in the waiting room.

The gift baskets include non-perishable foods like packets of cheese crackers, fruit, maybe some healthy muffins or bagels, individual serving cans of fruit or vegetable juice, non-refrigerated puddings and spoons, and up-to-date magazines. I try to avoid including nut products, due to possible allergies of others in the waiting room.

If I know a person's favorite foods I include some of them, too. I bring a lot because people often want to share these with others in the waiting room.

I package everything in an insulated tote bag. You can get it from the grocery store, or get a nicer one elsewhere.

Many people hesitate to leave the waiting room in case the doctor comes by, or their loved one takes a turn for the worse. Having food available is really helpful.

In one community where I lived volunteer groups would bring free hot meals to the waiting room for whoever was there. It was really appreciated!

–Katie Schwartz

Give "Juicy" Gifts of Health

As a nutritionist, I've seen fresh juices work MIRACLES.

There are combinations of veggie and/or fruit juices that taste ahh-some!

Juices require much less energy to digest, which are ideal for patients who are recovering. Fresh juices "mainline" the body with nutrients, vitamins, and minerals and have numerous health and emotional benefits. Yes, I've even seen people come out of a depression by drinking nature's remedies.

Fresh juices make a great care package. Google "fresh juices" for numerous services that will deliver or ship directly to the person. Shipping prices are now very reasonable, around $15 for over night Fedex to deliver many days worth of juices.

Many health food stores also have fresh juices. It's best to get fresh, cold-pressed, organic juices.

ALERT: If the juices aren't fresh, they may have sugar added and artificial ingredients. Those are NOT what you want! You want only nature's PURE fruit and/or veggie squeezed juices—nothing else added.

Watch them drink their troubles away . . . with fresh juices!

–Elaine Wilkes
Nutritionist

Awesome Thing to Do!

Community Knitting

Speaking of waiting rooms . . . This waiting room leaves yarn for anyone waiting to help knit a baby sweater that's given to the local orphanage.

Bring Food

I have a very dear friend whose husband was diagnosed with terminal melanoma. He was in and out of the hospital, and had enormous problems with side effects from surgery and chemotherapy. One of his biggest issues was his lack of appetite—nothing interested him.

When she told me this, I immediately drove down to our favorite restaurant (Claim Jumpers). I bought soup, salad, chicken potpie, and chocolate cheese pie for dessert.

I drove this to their house, completely unexpected. Surprised the heck out of them! They were appreciative, but I could tell they thought I'd wasted my money because he wasn't eating.

I talked with her the next night. She was nearly in tears. She said that he had eaten almost everything! It was the first real meal he had eaten in weeks.

I don't know what inspired me to do this, except the certainty that it was the right thing to do.

–Sharna Alt,
Veterinarian

At Home Recovery Food

Once home, make them a meal and just bring it to them. Don't ask, just 'do it.'

–Karen and Leslie,
The Hug Sisters

Naturally we think it's also great to provide them with at least the recommended eight hugs a day! :-)

A fruit creation basket, or a bowl of fruit is a good idea for what to bring.

–Natasha Carmon,
Author

MealTrain.com

People ask, "What can I do to help?" The answer has always been to help them with a meal.

Over 130,000 people have organized a Meal-Train for someone who is going through an illness, surgery, or welcoming a new baby.

MealTrain.com is a FREE website that organizes home-cooked meals for friends, from friends. Scheduling makes it easier to increase the effectiveness and participation.

Providing each giver this information helps simplify the process so they can focus on supporting others with meals. So far, we have helped over 130,000 families receive over 1,300,000 meals. In fact, more than 2500 families receive a meal each night because of mealTrain.com.

–Michael Laramee,
Co-Founder of mealTrain.com

Serve Them Their Favorite Food

We had a small, elderly woman in our hospice unit with severe cardiac disease and a small bowel obstruction. She had a tube in her nose that extended down to suction out her stomach as nothing was going through her system.

After several days of waiting to pass on, she decided that she wanted a steak. A Prime Rib steak, no less! With a tube in her nose and a complete bowel obstruction!

Well, we figured out how to make her last meal exactly what she wanted.

Her son went to a steak house and obtained a major portion of Prime Rib and brought it to the unit for her.

She cut up that steak, chewed it, savored all of the fragrance, flavor and juices, and then spit out the meat. The tube in her stomach suctioned out all of the juices she swallowed so they didn't make her sick.

She and the family were totally satisfied that she was able to thoroughly enjoy this experience and she passed several days later—a content woman.

–Brenda Schetnan,
RN and writer

Cook Up Organic Smiles

Hospital food is pretty awful, in my opinion, and is a problem since the body needs extra healing nutrients when illness occurs.

So I make homemade organic healing foods for loved ones in the hospital. They are so appreciative, especially after enduring microwaved, bland, non-organic and nutrient-low hospital food.

Food really is medicine.

–Katie Strand,
Singer

Treat 'em with a Healthy Shake

H When my dad was in the hospital, I was shocked that the popular "doctor recommended" drink they were giving him contained a cheap protein, and way too much sugar.

I knew there had to be something better.

As a nutritionist I made it a mission to find a healthier ready-to-drink shake that tasted great.

After looking at many products I found ENU. It tastes the best by far, has the healthiest ingredients, and contains no added chemicals, or processed and artificial sweeteners.

It has a perfect blend of nutrients to help the body recover without loosing muscle. (Once you lose muscle it's extremely challenging to get it back.)

I then gave ENU to my 96-year-old neighbor who was losing weight because he had no appetite for food, but he could handle liquids. He LOVES it! I don't tell him it's healthy since he thinks it's a fast food milkshake. :-) Even his family has noticed that he looks healthier from his "milkshakes."

Enu has 25 grams of organic protein of whey from grass fed cows. There's also a little fermented non-GMO soy, which is the healthy soy, and NOT the cheap soy that's GMO (genetically modified) and is an isolate found in other drinks.

Go to Amazon and search for "ENU shake," to find out all Enu's benefits.

I take ENU with me when I travel, since it needs no refrigeration, to provide needed nourishment while I'm on the road - rather than resorting to fast food.

I contacted the company to offer super discounts to my readers. For great discounts on Enu, see:

http://www.ez.com/enudiscounts

"Just trust that everything is unfolding the way it is supposed to. Don't resist. Surrender to what is, let go of what was, and have faith in what will be."

— Sonia Ricotti

Practical, Easy, Helpful Ideas

"It makes no sense to worry about things you have no control over because there's nothing you can do about them, and why worry about things you do control?

The activity of worrying keeps you immobilized."

—Wayne Dyer

Send Fun Cards

I have a pet lovebird named Luigi who shreds paper into precision strips with his beak. He's really dedicated to his work!

Recently, wanting to think of a way to showcase Luigi's talent (other birds shred paper, but they mangle it), I started making figurative collages out of the paper Luigi shredded. :-)

Yes, I got ridiculed quite a bit.

Last September, Luigi and I were on CBC's *Dragon's Den* (Canadian version of ABC's *Shark Tank*) and actually got a deal with one of the investors – an unexpected long shot!

When Joey, a boy dying of cancer, was asked what was his favorite all time pitch from *Dragon's Den* was, he immediately said, "Luigi!"

When I heard this, I hastened to send Joey special greetings from Luigi the Lovebird. I heard it cheered Joey before he died six days later.

It made me think that maybe other children would like to receive a special, personal card from a bird.

So every week I now send a Luigi card to a sick kid somewhere in North America.

Watch Luigi at: http://www.handandbeak.com

–Mary McQueen (and Luigi)

See special coupon code offer in back of the book for Luigi cards.

Send Card Cheers from Schoolmates

I had a major operation to remove my spleen when I was nine years old. My third grade teacher made my day a little brighter by having each student create a handmade card to wish me well. The cards were made out of construction paper and crayons.

I will never forget how happy the cards made me feel. I kept them in a manila envelope on my bed (so I could look through them repeatedly), and reminded myself that I was still a part of the class and I was loved.

–Josephine Bila, M.S.W.,
Emotional Wellness Consultant

Send Hand Written Cards

I remember recovering from a series of shoulder surgeries that made me homebound and isolated.

I recall how nice it was to get a card or note from anyone. That's why I started the WOES ministry at my church. WOES stands for Words of Encouragement and Support.

We send handwritten note cards to folks who are sick and shut-in just to let them know we are thinking about them.

It's a simple gesture that's appreciated by someone recovering from a broken ankle, massive stroke, suffering from depression, or is terminally ill.

–Holy Wolf,
Chief Marketing Officer

One of my girlfriends had her 10 year-old son hospitalized for medication adjustments. While he was in the hospital I helped my children write letters and make cards for him.

I know it is a simple gesture, but cards and letters mean a lot in today's tech savvy world. Besides, when you're feeling down a hand written card shows that someone is thinking of you and wishing you feel better!

–Crystal Zobel

It's In the Cards

My son slipped and fell onto one of the sharp points on top of the fence, piercing the flesh between his armpit and right shoulder.

I encouraged family and friends to send cards.

One of the cards, signed by all his classmates and teachers, brought a smile to his face. It simply said: "Everyone at school misses you and hopes you feel better soon."

–Cherry-Ann Carew

Therapy Dogs to The Rescue

"What made my day in the hospital was to have a service dog visit, lie down on my bed, and snuggle with me for a little while."

-Stel Fine

Dogs have an abundance of love to give. They seem to brighten everyone's day, and are usually a guaranteed feel-good visitor!

Here are a few services to contact that will bring a dog to the facility (hospital, nursing home, hospice, and other facilities) for FREE!

Therapy Dogs International

http://www.tdi-dog.org/

Doctors and administrators recognize the health benefits the visits can provide.

Individuals who are awaiting major surgery, are depressed, or have not had a visitor in a while can all be comforted and reassured by a visit from a gentle Therapy Dog. A friendly visitor with a wagging tail can make all the difference in the world.

Contact :
www.therapydogs.com, call 877-843-7364,
email: therapydogsinc@qwestoffice.net.

Other Therapy Dog services:

Pet Partners, Phone: 425 679-5500,
http://www.petpartners.org/

Pet Partners is the leader in promoting and demonstrating that positive human–animal interactions improve the physical, emotional and psychological lives of those we serve.

Bright and Beautiful Therapy Dogs,
Phone: 888-PET-5770
http://www.golden-dogs.org/

Therapy Dogs Incorporated
http://www.therapydogs.com/

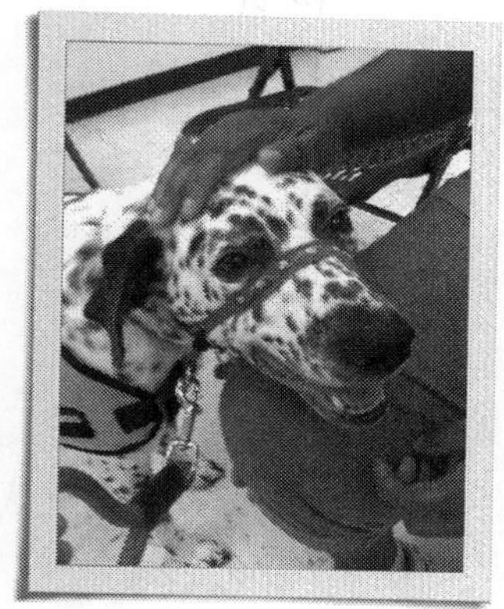

Or, ask if there's a pet therapy program at the facility. Usually the director of volunteers will know how to contact a member.

You can also Google "Therapy Dog," with your city and state in the search box to find dog services in your area.

Many rehab and nursing homes allow the patient's pets to come and visit, too.

Put a Lid on It

Sometimes it's hard for a patient to drink from a cup. They may not have the strength to sit up and drink, or the liquid may spill.

A great idea is get them a sippy cup, or water bottle that has a cap with a flip-up spout or straw. It's so much easier to drink from and avoids spills.

Or, check out the *Wow Cup* that automatically seals for no spills. It's made to be a rehabilitative and assistive drinking system. Their cups reduce the risk of spillage whether a person is lying down, sitting, or standing. It's 100% BPA & Phthalate free and made only from the safest food-grade plastic materials.
http://bit.ly/19VkcGs

It sounds simple, but it really helped taking care of my grandmother.

You'll want to keep the patient hydrated especially since meds can be very constipating.

–*Beth Crystalis,* Mother of three children

Get Them Moving

What you don't use—you lose, so help them get moving.

Many problems stem from the patient lying down too long without moving.

Doctors now realize it's vital to get the patient moving. After my mom's surgery, even when she was half asleep, nurses would wake her to sit up and dangle her feet, so she wouldn't be lying flat so long.

I saw three nurses help lift one man so he could sit up because they didn't want him lying flat all day and night. Then they would help move his body.

Another man went into emergency surgery because his gut atrophied from not being moved enough.

Always ask the staff about the appropriate

movement for the patient first. Sometimes they'll be more apt to move if you move with them, or assist them in their exercise. Can you get them walking? Can you get them to lift small weights? You can do simple things like getting them to point and flex their feet to help pump their circulation.

Another simple exercise is to squeeze and hold their buttocks for six seconds, and then repeat many times.

Any recommended movement is helpful to their recovery, and can also help improve their moods.

–Claudia Kelly
Physical Therapist

Clean the Clutter and Open the Window

Being in a messy room can make anyone feel exhausted.

To help, straighten the room — put away things on the table, throw out garbage, extra papers, take-out food containers, coffee cups, and newspapers.

The air can get stale in a sick person's room, so open the window to let in some fresh air, even if it's just for a few minutes.

You can also take essentials oils, and put in a spray bottle of water to mist the air. If gives such a nice relaxing scent, and helps with various emotions depending on the oil. For instance, lavender gives them relaxation, lemon can energize them.

When they leave for rehab or tests you can clean or straighten up the room, or get the cleaning staff to clean it. You can also open the windows to air it out.

It's so much nicer and easier to recover in a tidy room.

When they're home you could use an air cleaner or ceiling fan to circulate the air. An air cleaner helps remove viruses from the air so one is less apt to the catch flu and feel worse. We've noticed how our air cleaner detects the changes in the air after we cook. The red light will go on to show there's something in the air that needs to be cleaned. After extensive research, I'm happy with the Bio GS Air Cleaner by Rabbit Air.

–Michele Martin,
Dog sitter

Use Superfood Coconut and Coconut Oil Massage

Foods that have an incredible array of health benefits that go well beyond just their nutrient value are considered 'superfoods.' Mother's milk is considered the most perfect food because of its ideal nutritional content and immune boosting compounds. The closest match to mother's milk is found within the coconut, which is loaded with many powerful fatty acids that give it a unique taste and an abundance of health enhancing benefits. (Google coconut oil benefits to understand all the reasons why it's so beneficial.)

Recommended amount of coconut oil one should consume daily: Start with a teaspoon a day.

Put Coconut Oil on Your Skin

Many very sick patients gag when anything is put into their mouth, so rub it into their skin instead.

These MCT's (medium chain triglycerides) are also known for their ability to speed the healing process of cuts and bruises by destroying dangerous microbes, and enhancing cellular metabolism and tissue repair. It's also very soothing and great at reducing stress when it is applied onto face, temples, and scalp.

Look for organic varieties without preservatives that are available at most health food stores.

–Dr. Jockers,
Maximized living doctor

Find Out What They Want

Ask. Ask. Ask.

Ask the person:
What's your favorite color?
What types of magazines and books do you like?
What's your favorite snack? Favorite foods?
(Be sure that their diet is not restricted!)

That way you're bringing what they want and like.

Also, ask them how you can help. Ask what they'd like from you.

–Lorraine Milton,
Author

Wrap them in Warmth

When people are sick they often feel very cold. To warm them up, put their top sheets or blankets in the dryer.

Depending on the dryer temperature, in minutes remove the toasty sheets or blanket from the dryer. Then wrap them in warmth. Ahhh! You can put a blanket on top to keep the warmth in.

Many nursing homes have a washer and dryer.

Warm sheets feel great and very relaxing! Aaaahhh!

–Lily Hills,
Author and speaker

Schmooze the Hospital Staff

When my dad was in the hospital last year, I bought huge baskets of baked goods and left them in his hospital room.

If any person, nurse or therapist came to help him with his care, he was able to offer them a little treat.

Eventually, the staff was just stopping by his room to say, "Hi" and pay him a visit. He really enjoyed the company!

Oh yeah, don't forget the evening shift! Make sure you have enough goodies for the entire hospital staff.

–Edna Ma,
MD, board certified anesthesiologist

(Check the person's food restrictions. Sugar is not a good choice for diabetics or cancer patients.)

When my newborn daughter was in the ICU for five weeks, one of my friends came up with the idea to do something for the nurses, which was a great way to connect with them.

Over Easter, she and her daughter baked and decorated cookies for them. It was appreciated. We got the opportunity to talk in an informal way with the nurses caring for our daughter. That helped us build a more personal relationship with them.

–Kimberly Friddle,
Public speaker

Remember The Little Things

When I was hospitalized for an extended period of time, I was virtually alone. I'd just moved to New York by myself, while all my family was in Florida.

The security guard saw this, and one day brought me one small flower. I almost cried.

Over a year later, when one of my best friends left cross-country to pursue his dreams, he was alone and depressed. He was hospitalized for a suicide attempt. Despite the three hours difference in time, I stayed on the phone with him all night until he fell asleep.

Even the little things matter so much.

–April Dawn Ricchuito

"The best of healers is good cheer."

— Pindus

Making it Super Special

"You can't live a perfect day without doing something for someone who will never be able to repay you."

-John Wooden

Prepare Romance

My parent's 47th wedding anniversary was approaching and it was apparent that my father, who was hospitalized for an extended time would not be home in time for it. My sister and I talked to the nursing staff to arrange an awesome date.

We ordered a nice dinner from a local restaurant. We brought in flowers, a nice tablecloth, and candles.

The staff let us set up our meal at a table in the Physical Therapy area.

When it was dinnertime, we wheeled my dad to the "Dining Room" along with my mother. We then left them alone to enjoy a quiet dinner together to celebrate and, give my parents a special memory during a difficult time.

–Kathy A. Eubanks,
Speaker and author

Create a Fun Treasure Hunt

I was just about to attach the 'Nancy's Day' sign to the window of the mini when Nancy (who had terminal cancer) suddenly appeared at the car before I knew it! Nancy was so excited! She was like a school girl and started giggling straight away. Suddenly, the day really was exciting.

We drove down the drive and stopped at the tree where Nancy leapt out to have her photo taken with Alison's poster and the 'H' I gave her to hold. She had a smile from ear to ear and looked really well.

We arrived at Brenda's, who had prepared a wonderful breakfast of coffee, croissants, delicious toast and jams. We were having such a good time it was hard to tear ourselves away! Brenda gave Nancy a small picture frame in which she had hand painted a "D."

Nancy turned to me and said, "If my day ended here it would be just perfect." That was fabulous to hear as it meant we were on track!

Then, we went into a little bookshop where the owner handed Nancy a beautifully wrapped package. It contained a carved ceramic 'N' made by Becky.

We moved from there to the Woodstock museum where I was supposed to plant an 'A' amongst the sculptures. I had to think fast, so I suggested we look at the church.

What a choice! It's a simply beautiful church. A man played "Jesus Joy of Man's Desires" on the violin for us from the front pew. It turned out to be Nancy's favorite. Spooky!

I placed a large gold 'A' on the pew at the back of the church. I saw her smile when she discovered it.

Now she had H,A,D, and N, and she was intrigued. We then walked into Blenheim Palace where she struggled to walk down the riverbank.

Suddenly I thought I might have done this

wrong. When I asked her if she was okay, I received an enthusiastic nod and great big smile.

As we walked past some overhanging trees, we saw John and Paul with a picnic table and an open bottle of champagne ready to greet us.

As if by magic, the rather grey day changed to bright blue skies, and the sun peeped through in time for our wonderful picnic.

Milly had given me a bottle of Blenheim champagne and a montage of pictures making an 'E'. Nancy now tried to work out the word puzzle.

The picnic was superb. Then Paul produced a beautiful cake that Anita made in the shape o fan 'L'.

Now we had all the letters we needed, but Nancy had no clues.

I gave her a lovely card with a bear on it that said, "You saw a painting you loved which was called 'Swept Away.' Now you have a toy bear called Handel."

It was love at first sight and Handel was to become her close friend and confidante.

After we finished our picnic Nancy and I made our way slowly up the steps to the front of the palace. She found it tough going and I really felt for her, but she kept on smiling.

I waved goodbye to her as Paul drove her home. She was grinning from ear to ear.

What a day, what a lady.

–Jan Harvey,
Artist

Create a Heart Garden"

I'd been friends with Nancy for eight years. I knew when we met that she had cancer. It was like a condition of friendship; I have this thing and if we are to be friends, you have to live with it, too.

I accepted the conditions, and at her husband's suggestion I made myself "head of distraction," creating experiences that we would remember and laugh about for ages afterwards.

Then she died.

Just like that.

When I received the call, I was in a pub. My lunch was about to be served when my mobile buzzed.

I knew instinctively what had happened. My whole body froze. Naturally, it was a bad connection. I could hear only intermittently "Nancy .

. . hospital . . . this morning."

I felt every last part of my body go numb.

Suddenly, the world was too bright and far too busy.

I really needed people to rally round me, but strangely they didn't. There were no calls, cards, emails—not even texts. Everyone was too busy.

My cousin Jill flew in from Canada and it all seemed such a blur. Gin and tonics were mixed, cookies baked, and my son taken care of. Plus, I was given space to grieve.

Eventually, a friend called, the first in seven days. "How are you?" she asked. I told her I was still very upset, "What, still?" she replied.

Rattled, I took my dog to a large arboretum. The autumn colors were magical. I walked and walked crisscrossing the woods until I was exhausted. Then I sat under a tree and wept until there were no more tears.

When I came home I saw a big, shiny red heart hanging on the garden gate. It had "I Love you Mum" written on it. I half cried and half laughed.

Then, I opened the gate and realized that the entire garden path was decorated with glittering, shiny hearts that hung from all the bushes and trees, each singing with a message.

"I love you because you are funny."
"I love you because you are caring."
"I love you because you feed me." (That was from the dog.)

Every heart was different. Jill and my son had created a "Garden of Hearts."

As I stood there with an armful of hearts, Nancy's voice was coming to me again. Then I felt her there, in her favorite red jacket, throwing her head back and laughing.

–Jan Harvey,
Artist

Create a Box of Praises

A few years ago my mother was having serious health issues, and there was really nothing she needed or wanted for her 81st birthday.

So, to brighten her spirits, I took fancy paper and cut it into 2" x 5" strips. I put six strips in an envelope with a letter and sent it to every family member and friend I could find.

I asked them to write one short positive or funny memory they have of my mother on each strip, sign their name, and mail the strips back to me.

I then put them all in a mahogany box with a gold plate engraved "Our Memories of You," and gave the present to her. She cried and laughed reading all 100+ of the powerful notes. The perfect gift!

Praise Audio

When my mother became legally blind, and could no longer see those great notes, I purchased an app for my iPhone and read all 100+ messages into this app. I then converted it to an MP3 and uploaded it to iTunes. I then put it on an I-pod for her with a head set, so she can hear it without bothering anyone. Now she can have fun listening to what everyone said about her any time she wants! *(You can also audio record people for free saying their comments on Simple-VoiceBox.com.)*

Throw a Party!

Now she's in a nursing home, and is partially deaf, legally blind, and needs a feeding tube.

When it was her birthday again, we brought someone in to do her hair and give her a manicure and pedicure.

(Note: Check with the facility first since they may offer pedicures, or have restrictions about getting pedicures.)

Next I put an ad in the newspaper, with a good picture of her, wishing her happy birthday from her entire family. People were calling and telling her they saw the picture, which made her feel like a celebrity.

That day I told her to be dressed nice at 5:00 pm on her birthday because I had a surprise for her. I reserved a "community room" at the nursing home (since we could not take her out), decorated it with balloons and streamers, and had the family arrive, including two from out of state she had not seen in many years.

I treasure all these memories.

–Nancy D. Butler,
CFP®, CDFA™, CLTC

Give Them a Concert

When I was a hospice volunteer one of my clients loved music and had season tickets to the symphony. When she became too ill to attend a concert, I thought about getting a gurney so she could stay in the back of the auditorium, but that didn't work out.

So I asked the Conservatory of Music if they had a student who would be willing to play for a dying lady.

They sent over a violinist who gave a private concert for the woman and her family. They all agreed that it was the best musical event they ever attended.

–Allen Klein,
MA, Author

Create a Lending Library

When purchasing audio programs intended to improve or enhance health and life quality, I purchase an additional copy, which I provide to my primary care physician at his medical office.

The donation of these audio programs has created a "lending library" of audio CDs that are lent out to patients who are dealing with a variety of illnesses or life situations.

When patients are finished listening to the material, they return the CDs to the office to be lent out again to others.

The lending library currently consists of material by speakers and experts such as Wayne Dyer, Tony Robbins, Brendon Burchard, Stuart Wilde, Anita Moorjani, John Harrichurran, Steve Jones, and so on.

The physician reported that patients enjoy the material. It has helped them, and we look forward to expanding the library!

– Giovina Taraschi

Have Others Plant a Garden

I started *Hope in Bloom,* a non-profit program, after I lost a childhood friend and gardening buddy to breast cancer.

Hope in Bloom operates on a very simple model: Volunteer landscape architects or designers develop a garden plan after meeting with the recipient. Hope in Bloom purchases plants and materials, and a group from our 850 volunteers installs the garden at the home

of a breast cancer patient living in Massachusetts. To date, our volunteers have planted 120 gardens across the state.

So few people understand the power of nature and how much it can mean to all of us. Being exposed to greenery is especially important for those who are faced with illness.

Plant a garden and bring joy to someone going through a difficult time.

–Roberta Dehman Hershon

Awesome Thing to Do!

To brighten anyone's day, hand-deliver a bouquet of colorful flowers from your garden, or a collection of wild flowers. Bringing nature into a room is like sunshine for the soul.

Lift Their Spirits with a Tea Party

A young woman in our church was pregnant with twins and required hospitalization to prevent losing them. She was fearful and down in the dumps, so I brought her a tea party . . . picnic basket with teapot, china cups, scones, fruit, cheeses—the works!

I even brought her a hat and boa. She talked about it for years.

–Ann Bass,
CRTS

Awesome Thing to Do!

A box of their favorite tea makes a nice inexpensive gift.

Give Life

With her 42 year-old heart, lungs, and kidneys failing, my girlfriend almost died at Christmas in 2010.

Extensive testing and monitoring over many days in the hospital revealed that her kidneys were basically dead. She was going to have to live the rest of her life on dialysis.

We enjoyed pretty active lives, and overnight dialysis treatments were not much of a prospect for life. So I said I'd give her a kidney if I could.

Over the next few months, she went to work at 7am each day as usual, but only came home for dinner, and then off to the clinic for seven hours of overnight dialysis.

I had to keep pestering the hospital for months to see if I was a suitable donor.

It turned out we are a compatible couple in a way we could never imagine. On Sep. 23, 2011, my left kidney moved to its new host body.

To go with her new kidney, I also gave her a t-shirt that says, "I like to have a male organ in me all day."

I don't have health or life insurance, so I kept my 11-year-old son out of school the day before surgery to explain the risks. I reminded him of things I'd taught him, and reinforced how much I loved him.

Now, we are happily nearing the second anniversary of the transplant.

–Steve Chard,
President of YWPD - Internet Authority

Decorate a Miniature Christmas Tree

The doctors told us my grandmother was dying and that she would not be returning home.

Since it was Christmas, my grandmother's favorite time of year, a co-worker thought it would bring cheer to make her a beautifully decorated miniature 12-inch tall Christmas tree.

Sonji used her glue gun to put on ornaments. It even had real blinking Christmas lights.

I put it in the window of the hospital room and my grandmother lovingly stared at it as her final days neared.

Although it was cold outside, the warmth of that Christmas tree, surrounded by the love of family and friends in that hospital room, made the last-few days with my grandmother beautiful.

–Bridget Sims Lewis

Make a Snowman

When I was young, and my great aunt was dying, my brother and sister filled a trashcan with snow and brought it into her room. They built a miniature snowman on my aunt's tray table.

They then had a small snowball battle with her.

The staff at the nursing home wasn't happy, but it was one of the last laughs my aunt had.

So anything out of the ordinary that helps the patient smile or laugh is good.

– *Walter Meyer,*
co-creator Gam3rCon

Wacky Wednesdays

While going through a bone marrow transplant after a leukemia relapse, my 15 year-old daughter was missing spirit week at school, which included "Wacky Wednesday."

I hadn't seen her precious smile or light in her eyes for weeks. At the mere suggestion that we could create a Wacky Wednesday in the hospital she lit up like a Christmas tree.

As a result, our stress and sorrow was replaced with silliness and smiles.

A simple milk mustache, or painted on uni-brow is enough to lift spirits and create fun day in the hospital.

I've been dressing Wacky every Wednesday and visiting patients as a tribute to my daughter's legacy, and persevering passion to make the dream of having Wacky Wednesday in many facilities a reality!

–Denise Taylor,
Speaker, author

Play Imagination Games

When people aren't feeling well, it's so much easier to think about what's wrong than what could get better.

There are numerous studies on how visualization can help people.

Here's visualization on steroids . . .

Use the concept of the "come as you wanna be" parties with B.Y.O.D.—Bring Your Own Dreams.

When a bell went off, everyone would act like it's a year from now, and talk about how splendidly (well, healthfully, magnificently, miraculously) the last year went—meaning the year coming up.

It's important to plant the instruction early about only discussing the positive aspects of "the last year." Otherwise, people can reinforce their old negative stories even more firmly.

The purpose was to get people to believe a great year already happened. It also made them open to fresh ideas.

The energy of the party is very upbeat, with everyone talking about their future successes as if they're happening now.

Play this game with the person who's sick. Have a conversation like it's one year from now. Talk about how they recovered so well. How they feel so good. Why they had such a speedy recovery. If you really play the game, it can be fun, but also provide enormous insight, along with bringing hope and new possibilities.

–Andrea Sholer,
Personal Coach

Bring Pictures

I always tell the families of elderly patients, or patients who have head injuries, to bring pictures of their loved ones to the hospital and hang them up in their room. It's human nature to look at older people and head injured people as . . . well . . . old people and head injured people.

There's a disconnect, and the communication factor is often diminished in some way. Old photographs from better days, like wedding pictures, photos of men in uniform, and graduation photos remind us that these patients were once like us.

If the patient is old, comatose, terribly disfigured, or can't communicate for some reason, bring a picture of that person when they were young and healthy. Place that picture in the room where everyone can see it.

This lets everyone see the real person inside the sick body. It reminds them that this could be their child or their mom. –*Barbara Bergin,* M.D.

Put Their Name on Prayer Lists

I often join friends from church to visit the sick, or people in the hospital, to help pray for them or cheer them up.

Praying for a sick person may be the best thing that you can do for him or her or their families.

Your presence in their moment of weakness can provide strength and encouragement. The divine presence in their lives can give supernatural power to aid in their ailing heart, spirit, and sick bodies.

–Carmen Campo,
Social Media Manager

Here's a list of prayer groups that will pray for the sick.

Silent Unity has an amazing 30 days of continuous prayer support. They can be reached 24/7 at 1-800-669-7729 and will also mail a letter if you wish.

www.csl.org
Sponsored by World Ministry of Prayer.

http://www.spiritualliving.org/services-support/prayer-support/

Or, they'll pray over the phone
http://www.unity.org/prayer

A prayer list:
http://www.msia.org/prayer

Many churches have prayer groups that will pray for the sick.

You can also call your local church and request a mass said for them.

Offer to Drive

A neighbor heard I needed to be in UCSD for treatment and appointments every week for seven months.

She cooked for me, and volunteered to drive me down for the one-day visits, three times a month. This was a clinical trial, and I believe I would have quit if she hadn't volunteered to help me because it was just too stressful.

–Lisa Guest

Awesome Thing to Do!

It may be good to go to their appointments with them and hear what the doctor has to say. Sometimes a patient may miss or misunderstand what the doctor said. You may help provide clarity for the patient.

Don't Ask, Just Do It

"Let me know if you need anything," is a common phrase.

When I was at my sickest I could barely get out of bed, but I'm not one to ask for help, or give someone a list of my needs, even when they asked if I needed anything.

What I appreciated most was when someone just showed up to help, or to bring me something to eat or drink.

Chances are people who are sick do need help with housekeeping, yard work, meal preparation, errands, transportation to medical appointments, possibly doing their bills, and even handling things like emails, phone calls, or writing thank you notes, but they might not ask for help.

So don't ask, just do it. If it's near a holiday, help them with decorating, shopping, gift-wrapping, and preparing a holiday meal.

It's also great to call and tell them you're thinking about them. Then tell them you have time on such and such day to help with chores or errands.

My sister sent someone to clean my house. My son came over on a regular basis to cut and trim the grass. Others offered to help, but I didn't ask for anything.

Also, the longer someone is sick the lonelier it gets. Friends aren't in contact as often and family gets complacent. Social isolation creeps in over time, which doesn't help with healing.

–Angil Tarach-Ritchey RN,
GCM. Eldercare Expert

It Takes a Village

If it takes a village to raise a child, it also takes a village to help a family whose life has been turned upside down by a traumatic incident. We continue to revel in the kindness of family and friends who are still helping us through this life change.

After Jim's accident, our friends and family were wonderfully and warmly supportive, offering assistance, prayers, and love and flying in from all over the country to be with us.

Some of the nicest and most thoughtful things people did included: Pitching in to hire a weekly cleaning service, arranging a sign-up schedule for people to bring meals, offering to take my sons to and from Drivers Ed and sports practice.

Our local friends here were fantastic and arranged meals for our family for about three months. They arranged for weekly maid service and took our dog to their homes during the day when I was at the hospital.

The visiting hours at the ICU were not convenient for a family with school-aged children, so friends signed on to visit my husband for the "late shift," 9 PM until 11 PM, to ensure someone would be with him when we could not. In fact, I was never alone at the ICU -- someone local from our family, neighborhood, or church would come sit with me in case something happened.

Later, several friends took turns coming to sit with my husband at home so I could go out for a while. People were so generous with their time.

We felt so lucky.

–Laura Ellison Cook

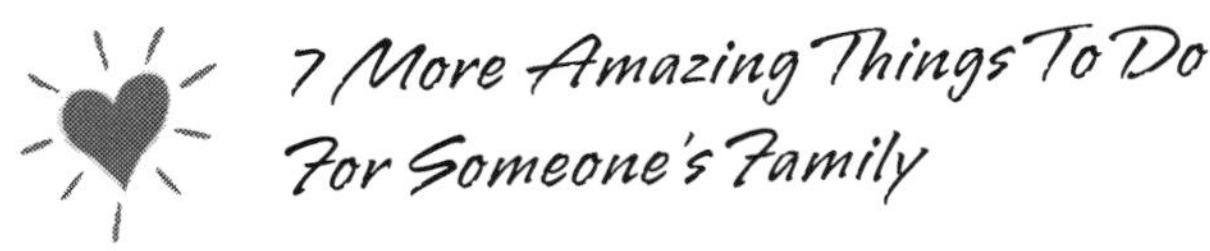

1) I've taken their children to the park, provided sleepovers, and cooked meals.

2) I've organized our social network to provide meals on a regular basis, so that cooking was a non-issue for the family.

3) I've arranged for house cleaning, laundry,

and carpools, so that my friend(s) in the hospital only had to focus on healing and getting well.

4) Because I am certified in reflexology, I have given my friends reflexology sessions, which help to enhance healing, balance energies, and provide relaxation. This is a gift my friends love.

5) When my husband was hospitalized I learned to do for my friends what wasn't done for me, and what would have been beneficial and extraordinarily helpful.

6) Since most people have a hard time asking for what they need, or may not even know what they need, it's important to ASK and then not feel obligated to do it all yourself, but put together a team.

7) Ultimately people want to be helpful, but don't always know what to do. It helps when someone coordinates and delegates. I've found that most people like to be given specific tasks.

–Loren Gelberg-Goff,
LCSW, Psychotherapist

"'Worry' is a word I don't allow myself to use."

—Dwight D. Eisenhower

Nurturing Ideas

"Too often we underestimate the power of a touch, a smile, a kind word, a listening ear, an honest compliment, or the smallest act of caring, all of which have the potential to turn a life around."

-Leo Buscaglia

Pamper Them

We're touch deprived! There are points on the forehead that when gently and lovingly stroked or held, can be very relaxing.

–Lisa Gironda Bailey,
LMT, RMP, Licensed Massage Therapist

Lovingly cradle the backs of their heads as they do in craniosacral therapy, where the head relaxes into one's palms. People report feeling so much better from this simple gentle gesture.

–Juliette,
Oncology Aesthetician

Awesome Thing to Do!

Think how a smell can bring you down memory lane. This is great for you and them! Breathe deeply with essential oils and oil blends to take you on a sensory journey that can instantly soothe, enliven, or balance both body and mind.

I recommend Young Living essential oils because they're pure, organic, therapeutic grade. Packed within these pure, botanical essences, you'll discover rich therapeutic properties that cannot be found elsewhere. Elevate your or their spirit, or promote mental clarity, or restore harmonic balance. Rub the oils on their feet, neck and shoulders. Their oil Panaway is great for relieving pain.

Give Foot Massages

Foot massages can be very relaxing, feel wonderful, reduce stress, increase circulation, and even help people sleep better.

It's amazing how it can even help reduce swelling of the feet. You'll see a noticeable difference with a regular massage.

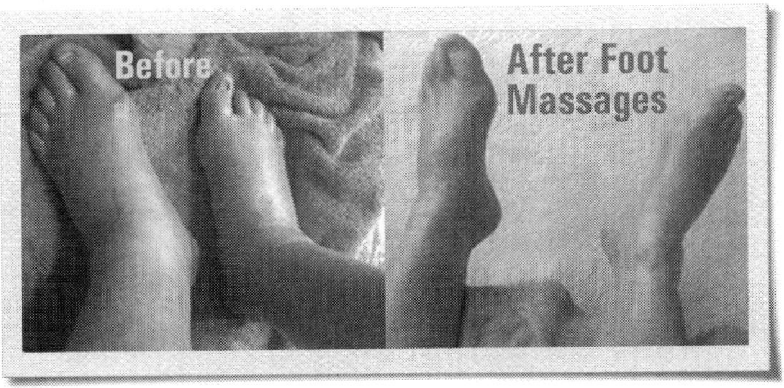

Foot massages can be done without oils, over their socks, or with oils like organic coconut or jojoba oil available at health food stores. Those are stable oils, while other oils may not hold a long shelf life and can become rancid.

Rub the foot towards the upper body.

Obviously, do not massage the foot if it's been injured.

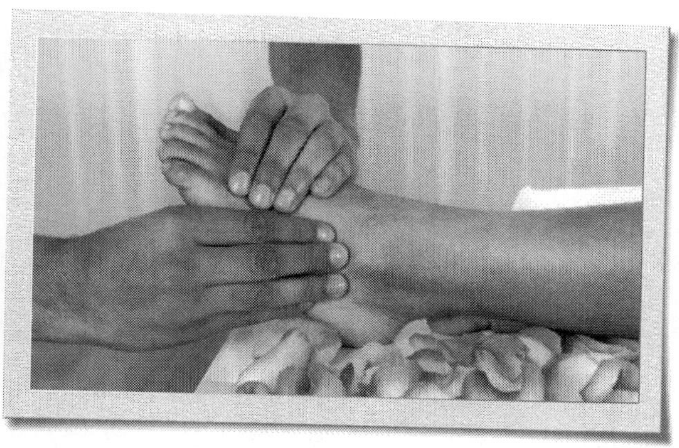

Awesome Thing to Do!

An awesome gift is a massage. A massage helps with depression, anxiety, improves sleep, promotes circulation, boosts immunity, eases pain, and feels great!

You can hire a professional to give a foot massage or full body massage. Always ask the doctor first to make sure it's okay. For example, if they had back surgery, they can't have their back or stomach massaged. So check first.

It's best to use creams or oils with natural ingredients and no chemicals.

"I am convinced that unconditional love is the most powerful known stimulant of the immune system. If I told patients to raise their blood levels of immune globulins or killer T cells, no one would know how. But if I can teach them to love themselves and others fully, the same changes happen automatically.
The truth is: love heals.

-Bernie Siegel, MD

Give Personal or Professional Grooming

An elderly family friend was in the hospital recovering from lung surgery. I visited him on a weekday night when no one else was there.

He told me he really wanted to wash his face and brush his teeth.

I got washing and brushing supplies from the staff. I filled the pink bucket with clean water, and helped him wash his face and brush his teeth. He said it felt so much better to be clean.

–Eileen Roth,
Author, Speaker, and Productivity Expert

Professional Grooming Service Treat

As an anesthesiologist I know the hospital both inside and out!

Recently a colleague of mine was put on bed rest due to preterm labor. I purchased an on-site manicure-pedicure service to have her nails done in her hospital bed. (Make sure you check with the facility to see if this is okay.)

Also check with your facility since some places provide these services.

I've seen people also order other professional grooming services for patients.

For men a good clean shave is nice because they start getting oily and stubbly after just a few days. It feels great to get cleaned up.

–Edna Ma,
MD, board certified anesthesiologist

One of the nurses and I turned the room into a hair salon. We kept Harvey in stitches. What a beautiful memory. That's what friends are for.

–Vickie Oldham

I visited a friend in the hospital who had been there for months, and gave her the full pamper works. Shaved her legs, massaged and exfoliated her feet, painted her toenails and gave her a manicure. It definitely cheered her up.

(Note. Make sure you ask first, since some patients are on drugs where if they bled or got scraped, it could result in complications.)

–Deborah Clemens

Awesome Thing to Do!

You can buy dry shampoo that can be used to clean their hair while they're in bed for extended times.

You can give a relaxing facial, or hire a professional.

Give Them Healing Touch

"Feel it in your heart—feel it in your hands."

Practiced by millions of people, "Healing Touch" emphasizes compassionate, heart-centered care. It restores harmony, energy and balance within the human energy system and supports the self-healing process of becoming whole in body, mind, emotion and spirit.

"Healing Touch" is used in a wide variety of settings including hospitals, long-term care facilities, private practices, hospices, and spas. Scientific studies also back this healing modality.

About "Healing Touch"

Janet Mentgen was a practicing nurse for 43 years developed "healing touch" methods.

Her research, private practice, and her teaching of energy medicine earned her the Holistic Nurse of the Year Award from the American Holistic Nurses Association in 1988.

In 1993, American Holistic Nurses Association (AHNA) certified Healing Touch.

What Happens in a Session

The individual lies fully clothed on a massage table while the provider gently places their hands slightly above or on the individual.

The session generally lasts 40 to 60 minutes, and people frequently report feeling deeply relaxed and peaceful during and after the session. There is a cumulative effect of using Healing Touch over time, and regular sessions are recommended.

You can practice Healing Touch, or to find a practitioner go to: http://bit.ly/18ew9Gz

However, here's a video to show you how to use Healing Touch yourself: http://bit.ly/baOXBy

"Compassion doesn't say, 'What can the world do for me?' but rather, 'How can I serve the world?' It is the feeling you access when looking at the world through the eyes of the divine heart."

—Debbie Ford, Author

Emotional Support

"Character cannot be developed in ease and quiet. Only through experience of trial and suffering can the soul be strengthened, ambition inspired, and success achieved."

-Helen Keller

Comfort Them During Their Last Hours

My friend, Brett, suffered from kidney failure and had had several transplants.

His greatest fear was being alone when his time came. His brother (and best friend) had passed away a couple of years earlier, his step-mom shortly after that, and his father was suffering from Alzheimer's. So, other than his sister-in-law and nephew, he really had no one but me.

I spent a lot of time with him as his body began to shut down, and I scheduled my vacation to coincide with the last week of his life to be with him. The day he died was one of the hardest things I've ever experienced, but it was also one of the greatest. He could no longer see or speak, but I knew that the hearing is the last of the senses to go, so I talked and sang to him as I softly stroked his arm and face.

I sang hymns and read passages from the Bible. He seemed very comforted by that. I realized he could hear me and knew what was going on because when his dad came into the room, I stopped singing to Brett to speak to his dad. Brett immediately became agitated. His body began to twitch and he was trying to speak. I began singing and stroking his arm again, and he quickly quieted down.

I stayed for six hours, just talking and singing quietly to him. He seemed very peaceful, and went quietly at the end. I wasn't sad because I knew it was what he wanted. I was grateful that I could be there for him to fulfill his one request that he not be alone at the end.

Two other close friends died alone in their hospital beds shortly before Brett died. I wish I had thought to do the same for them.

–Kim Westrope,
Office manager, writer

Spread Your Love

When we want to heal ourselves or help another do the same, we need to focus our thoughts on love, as it is the highest vibration.

If you're filled with this love when you go in to visit a patient, the patient will pick it up.

How to get there in thought and emotion, which will directly affect the physical body, is to go back into a time when you experienced extreme Joy and Light. This could be a place you traveled to, a celebration, marriage, or having a child. Whatever it is . . . go there in your mind and "feel" this light infusing into your entire being. Feel the elation and expansion in your heart.

Then create new healing thoughts such as:
"I want to feel like this in every cell of my being all the time."
"I want to feel this joy and create more love in my relationship."
Whatever you wish.

Keep the thoughts uplifted and when they

wander . . . just go into whatever memory will bring the light back into your heart to create healing for yourself and others around you.

When we call upon Infinite Light through Love and Gratitude we can direct it inwards to ourselves . . . and also touch another with that "Light."

–Leslie Sloane,
Creator of Auracle's Colour Therapy

Release Worry

"Worry does not empty tomorrow of its sorrow.
It empties today of its strength."
- Corrie Ten Boom

When my grandfather was sick my stepbrother was so consumed with worry that when he came to the hospital to visit it seemed like a black cloud had descended on the room. He was such a basket case he couldn't appreciate the importance of just being with my grandfather. It was exhausting and upsetting to be around my stepbrother.

I'd tell him his worry brings everyone down, including the patient. He'd say, it's in my genetics; that's what my family does. He honestly felt he had to worry, and he did a great job of it. His worry affected everyone, and spread faster than any virus in the hospital.

Fortunately, my grandfather recovered from both his illness and my stepbrother's gloom.

As a nurse, I see this over and over. It's as though people feel worry shows caring. It's not caring when you throw in drama and take worry to the extreme. It's your emotions running amuck and spreading all over everyone else.

My tip: Excessive worry makes the situation worse for everyone, so choose to release it. Be a comfort instead.

–Sandra Greenberg,
Nurse

Appreciate and Have Fun with Them NOW

When Joe was home again from the hospital we got everyone together to see him.

There were ten of us, and we ended up sitting in a circle. One person started by saying, “I’d like to share about Joe.” His authentic, heart-warming comments were filled with love.

Then spontaneously, one by one, we each told everyone why we loved Joe so much. We were all so touched. It was a magical evening that just happened without any planning. We were all in the flow. Joe soaked it all in and truly cherished everyone’s love.

Joe died a few moths later.

We were so grateful about the celebration of life we gave Joe. We talked about how wonderful it was for Joe to hear all those amazing comments while he was still alive.

There's so much hope and hoopla when a baby is born.

But, I think it's sad that when a person is sick and dying, there is lack of faith or hope — and no hoopla.

I recently helped a woman at her end of life. I encouraged her family to have a party, with balloons and all the gear, when she came home for her last few hours. They were so happy they did this.

–Jeanette Gallagher,
Radio Host

Give Them a Journal of Love

Darren Hardy, publisher of *Success* magazine, reveals an awesome gift that a person will cherish forever.

He gave this to his wife (who liked it better than the BMW car he gave her earlier that year), but you could use this simple idea for the person who's sick! It's guaranteed to brighten their day!

Every day, with a heartfelt focus, write in a journal one thing you like about the person who's sick (or for any special day like their birthday, anniversary, Christmas, or Thanksgiving).

Then give them the journal filled with all the things you love about them. You'll also feel good because every day you're directing your attention on what's good about someone you care about.

Use a Positive Approach

"There is one consolation in being sick; and that is the possibility that you may recover to a better state than you were ever in before."
—Henry David Thoreau

I learned that I could hasten my healing process if I focused on something other than the "woe is me" aspect of the difficulty.

I think developing a positive approach is the best gift you can offer someone undergoing a medical challenge.

Worry and wringing of the hands doesn't help anyone.

–Annette Langer,
Author

See Them Positively Healed

Here's a tip: See them whole, healed, surrounded in pure white light from the top of their head to the soles of their feet. Declare them healed in the name of (whatever higher power or religion you choose).

Have others pray for them and see them whole and healed and declare it. As a chiropractor, before I adjust anyone, I see their subluxations cleared and I see them healed.

–Dr. Jeffrey Ptak,
DC, MA.

Laughter is the Best Medicine

I had surgery to implant a spinal cord stimulator. Unfortunately, during the second procedure I came as close to dying as possible.

I was transferred to a nursing home and almost died again.

During this time, my dear friend and writing partner decided that the best thing she could do for me was to make me LAUGH.

Every night she would call me, and read these really funny vignettes she had written the previous day. And they were really funny!

I don't doubt for a second that my friend saved my life, and I firmly believe in the power of laughter as one of the most important aspects of the healing process.

These stories eventually became *Spoon and the Moon* (released as an app), which has been on the Amazon Bestseller list. (*Receive it for free. See back of book.*)

–Marie Davis and Margaret Hultz,
Wickedly Sisters
App Developers

When I've been sick, I appreciated company and conversation that's filled with laughter and light-heartedness.

Being serious and weepy didn't help me, or my loved ones when I was in the hospital. Bringing and reading funny articles or books is a huge help for healing. In fact, studies prove that laughter heals. It's not just because it makes people feel good, but because it affects body chemistry, and reduces acidity (stress/cortisol) in the body.

–Katie Strand,
Singer

My friend went ice-skating right before her wedding, and someone fell on her leg and broke her kneecap.

During a hospital visit I told her about the worst day of my life! It got her laughing so hard. It made her "time in the pen" much easier since she was otherwise so bored.

Flowers take up space, and they may not be able to read books because of the meds, so telling funny stories is the perfect remedy.

–Lara Fabans

"A hospital bed is a parked taxi with the meter running."

—Groucho Marx

Great Gift Ideas

"Each day provides its own gifts."

—Marcus Aurelius

Cute Hats with Natural Hair

Claudia's Cool Hats has a website that lets cancer patients choose a hat with hair that can easily disguise their hair loss.

These fashionable hats have 100% natural hair built in and make a great gift!

There are ten different hair color options available and nine different hairstyles. This hat will feel great and won't look like a fake wig.

Since it's natural hair a hairstylist can even cut the hair to match a certain style that the patient would like.

There are three styles. You can even choose a few different looks in order to have a variety of options to wear depending on the occasion or mood.

(*Discount at back of this book.*) Check out the website and see what looks you can create. http://www.claudiascoolhats.com

Awesome Thing to Do!

After her last bout of chemotherapy, she cut all her fluffy hair off before it fell out again. She filled her bird feeders with it and then watched all the nesting birds take it to give their nests the ultimate soft lining. The best kind of recycling!

iPads and Eye Pads

Keep Them Active with iPads

As part of the Rotary Club, we donate iPads for residents of the aged care and dementia ward. From crossword puzzles to reading newspapers in different languages, or game playing, to watching all types of videos — the iPads have provided the patients with a new avenue for entertainment and engagement.

This program has been in place for a number of months now, and has been an overwhelming success in patient care.

–Brad Butcher

Help Them Sleep with EYE Pads

Eye pads are another great idea because the staff often comes into the room in the middle of the night to check vitals. But, with eye pads covering their eyes patients won't be so startled when the harsh fluorescent lights flicker on.

See scented eye pillows that can be heated or cold that can also help with headaches or sinus issues at http://bit.ly/1hirc2F.

How's Their Pillow?

Some patients are in bed for so long, so it's important to make sure they have a wonderfully comfortable pillow.

Here are some helpful suggestions that you can find on Amazon.

One is a small cervical roll that can fit into any pillowcase next to the pillow. It gives terrific neck support. The name is Optp.com and it's around $20.

Give Them Your Message to Sleep On

Several years ago my young daughter Lauren was bullied by some 4th grade classmates, so she came home and made herself a comforting pillowcase that said, "I'M AWESOME."

As lifelong volunteers who've worked with many children, my friend Kris Faller and I thought Lauren had a good idea for comforting others, so we started a small company called UPPERCASES that digitally prints cotton pillowcases with bright graphics and positive messages.

I would often print cases as gifts for family and friends who were sick or in the hospital, so it made sense that our first retail customers were hospital gift shops.

Once we started personalizing the pillowcases and went online, we found that we often received orders for kids in pediatric hospitals. We also donate cases to the Ronald McDonald House and Home of the Innocents and are humbled by the notes we receive telling us how much our inspiring cases have helped others.

A little girl's idea has gone a long way.

–Ursula Robertson-Moore,
Co-owner of UPPERCASES

(Discount in back of this book.)

Give Fun Gowns or Stylin' PJs

During my first day of radiation, the nurse looked at me, pointed to the dressing room and handed me a hospital gown. She said, "You're going to wear one of these for the next seven weeks," and pointed to a stack of hospital gowns.

That was my "Vera Wang moment," when the kimono-style flannel gown was born. I knew I might not be able to control cancer, but I could control what I wore

The Best Therapy

I purchased the brightest cheerful flannel fabric I could find, and made a pattern to allow for drains, coverage and front opening. I designed it for dignity. I wore it the very next day of radiation.

Soon, I began receiving requests to make them for others.

The best part about it was it took the focus off me.

A hospital gown screams, "I am sick." A Hug Wrap makes them feel like they matter.

–Brenda Jones,
President of HugWraps.com

Awesome Thing to Do!

You may also consider giving them a nice bed jacket. It's a nice cover-up that only comes to the waist, so it's fine for lying in bed.

Someone who's bedridden for a while may also want some super fun PJs. The company P. J. Salvage (http://www.pjsalvage.com) has cute patterns, flannel, or velour PJs and robes with themes of sheep, ice cream cones, and many more cheerful images on them.

Give Your Miles

I cashed in miles and flew from Chicago to Pittsburgh to stay with Uncle Leo.

He never woke up while I was there, but I wanted the nurses to know about Leo, his infectious laugh and his loving ways.

So I wrote a note about how he was a grandpa and proud Minnesota farmer, and hung it on his ICU wall so they'd know who Leo truly was—and not just another patient.

–Karla (Krengel) Hood

Awesome Thing to Do!

Gift your airline miles to anyone who suddenly needs to go to be with a loved one who is ill.

Gift 'em with Hospital Gift Cards

When a close friend's son was in an out of town hospital for a risky surgery and subsequent stay, I arranged with the hospital to purchase a gift card (not something they normally offer) for their cafeteria, since I knew funds were tight for them, especially during that time.

I knew she would have gone without eating as she was unable to leave the hospital, so this helped relieve some of the stress for her.

–Melanie Koerperich

More Awesome Practical Gifts

One of the most thoughtful gifts I received when my husband was hospitalized was a large cheery floral tote with lots of pockets filled with books, notepads, pens, a camera, snacks, and more. I took to the hospital every day. See tote at: http://bit.ly/1g74flw

I also received several journals to record questions for the doctors and take notes on his progress.

Another friend sent me personalized stationary to use for my thank you notes.

We also appreciated all the cards, letters, emails, and Caring Bridge messages.

–Laura Ellison Cook

Battery Lit Candles

Make their room cozy and homey with battery lit, flameless candles. You can get a three-pack of pillar candles for around $11.

Find Something to Entertain Them

Last year, my mother was diagnosed with colon cancer just six months after my father died from complications of Alzheimer's disease.

As I rushed around her home grabbing the items she wanted (including her eyebrow pencil!) I spotted the cheap toy parrot my mom had named, Polly. With a push of a button, the parrot repeated everything you said. Originally designed for young children, these toys have proven effective in lifting the spirits of dementia patients. My father liked to talk to Polly even in the latter stages of Alzheimer's.

I tossed Polly into a bag. It was one of the best decisions of my life.

When Mom came out of surgery she was thrilled to see "her girl" and she didn't mean me. Mom would show off Polly to the nurses and record sweet things for them to hear. Interacting with the silly toy kept Mom's mind active, which is important after major surgery and anesthesia.

–Joy Johnston,
Health & Fitness Freelance Writer

"Mountains cannot be surmounted except by winding paths."

- Johann Wolfgang Von Goethe

Ideas from Patients

*"I find hope in the darkest of days,
and focus in the brightest.
I do not judge the universe."*

—Dalai Lama

Here's something I did for myself.

When I was diagnosed with breast cancer, every time someone sent me a loving message of support by email I pasted it into a Word document.

Then I printed out all those wonderful, loving messages, and that's what I read while I was sitting in the waiting room waiting for my scary appointments.

I took all that love with me, so I could focus on love instead of fear.

A friend read my love messages to me when I was waiting to go into surgery.

Sometimes people would include things in their messages that scared me. For example, they would say something like, "I know what you're going through because my aunt died of what you have." I wouldn't include the parts of their messages that scared me; I only copied and pasted the loving parts.

They held me through that entire scary experience that lasted the good part of a year.

–Randy Peyser,
Author

Awesome Thing to Do!

The wow factor: Collect these loving messages, and give them to brighten their day!

Looking Outside Yourself

I was in the hospital after suffering both a stroke and a brain tumor.

When the tumor was removed I was feeling pretty lousy, but believed that if you can think of and help others you are less likely to worry about yourself, and your recovery will be faster.

A patient next to me had her curtains drawn all the time, so I never saw her. That night I heard her crying, and I asked the nurse to offer her my crystal angel that a friend had given me to look after me while I was in hospital. "Tell her she can borrow my angel tonight and it will keep her safe."

The lady accepted it, and the next day she opened her curtains and began talking to me. She opened up her heart, and I was able to talk and listen to her.

When two people are suffering a similar illness

they can understand each other because they are experiencing similar emotions, so they're more likely to open their hearts to each other.

We became good friends. I felt gratified that even when I was suffering and unable to get out of my bed, I was still able to do something kind for someone who was also facing her demons.

–Barbara Gabogrecan

Keep Hope and Embrace the Gains

In 1997 Chris Berry, a 17 year-old boy, was critically injured when he was hit by a thief in a stolen car while he was walking his girlfriend home.

I contacted his mother through the *Star Ledger*, and told her my personal survival story to show how important it is for her not to lose hope in her son's full recovery.

I went with his mother and family to the rehab center to meet Chris in person. I told them, "Four days before my high school graduation in 1979 when I was 17 years old, I was literally DOA from a serious car accident. After 6 months in a coma, the doctors had little hope for my survival. But survive I did, as a bedridden cripple in the prime of my life."

I faced the loss of the use in my left arm and leg, and damaged eyesight. This was accompanied by the demons of depression, fear, inferiority, and lack of self-esteem.

This debilitating injury, combined with the uncertainties of adolescence, led to a serious bout of clinical depression, self-pity, and self-loathing.

Through years of soul-searching, reading philosophers such as David Hume, John Locke, and the works of Confucius, I developed a philosophy of endurance and positive attitude by learning to disregard my losses—and embrace my gains.

I began writing motivational poetry to inspire other people to achieve a level of higher being. I became a motivational speaker for support groups, using my personal experience to teach others how to overcome feelings of inadequacy.

I seriously believe that my life was spared so I could use my tragedy to help others with tragedies in their lives

Just as a gem cannot be polished without friction,
a man cannot be perfected without trials.
-Confucious

–Charles Breitweiser,
Motivational speaker, author

"I told my doctor I broke my leg in two places.
He told me to quit going to those places."

- Henny Youngman

Final Thoughts

"If the world were perfect, it wouldn't be."

—Yogi Berra

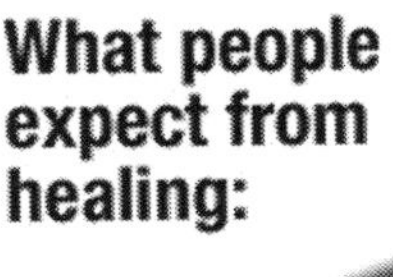

There may be days that aren't as good as the previous day, or it may feel like nothing is happening.

A "bad" day doesn't mean it'll stay "bad" forever. It may be part of the journey to healing.

Ways to Help Natural Pain Relief and Healing

There are natural alternatives to pain pills that don't have side effects that you may wish to check out.

Cold Laser and Electrical Stimulation

Dr. Oz aired a show about cold laser for natural pain relief.
http://bit.ly/WX6eeH

Some health professionals combine 20 minutes of cold laser, with 20 minutes of electrical stimulation, and 20 minutes of ultrasound for pain relief.

Do an Internet search about AWT-Acoustic Wave Therapy to help with pain. Many people have had fantastic results with this natural FDA approved therapy. It also helps greatly with removing cellulite and firming the face and body. But it needs to be done consistently for the physical results.

Eliminate Sugar

Eating sugar causes inflammation, which can greatly increase your pain. If you want less pain, eat less or no sugar.

The latest research shows that white processed sugar and high fructose corn syrup are some of the biggest culprits that affect all types of illness.

There are many tasty NATURAL alternatives to sugar. RAW honey (processed honey doesn't have the nutrients of raw honey), coconut sugar, and stevia are a few. Some experts aren't sure about agave.

Emotional Techniques

Science is discovering that one's emotions can either help or hinder healing.

Many people have found the various techniques listed below are extremely helpful. They all have online and in-person courses that you may want to check into. There are no negative side effects.

- GoUSM.edu
- TheWork.com (Her CD titled, *Loving What Is,* is excellent for stressful times.)
- TheTappingSolution.com
- TheSedonaMethod.com

See more awesome product, book and audio recommendations at:

101AwesomeThings.com
ElaineWilkes.com
facebook.com/101AwesomeThings

Family Bonding

We developed a family motto that my sons and I would huddle together and say to each other as we faced down this adversity: "We are Cooks, we are strong."

In addition, I made it very clear to my teenaged boys that under no circumstances would any of us use this situation as an excuse to engage in negative behavior and/or become less vigilant about maintaining goals, integrity, and family rules. In other words, stay on track, no backsliding.

We've remained a strong family team, helping my husband/their dad, supporting each other, and staying positive about the future.

–Laura Ellison Cook

It's Going to Be Okay

My high school buddy Rocky had a very close relationship with his grandfather who raised him. They were like best friends, always fishing or going to Red Sox games together.

Then Rocky's grandfather was diagnosed with cancer. Given only two weeks to live, Rocky and his grandfather were devastated. His grandfather was afraid to die. "I'm not ready to die," he confided in Rocky.

Rocky tried his best to comfort his grandfather. He visited him in the hospital, doing everything he could to make his final days as bearable as possible.

Then one day he walked into his grandfather's room and saw his grandfather smiling.

"I had a dream," the grandfather told Rocky, "These elves came down this bright tunnel and told me it was okay to join them."

He then looked up at his grandson and said, "It's going to be okay, Rocky."

Rocky's grandfather passed shortly after that — with a smile on his face.

–David C. Ladner

About the People Who Shared Their Stories

Some offer awesome deals.

1. **Laura Ellison Cook**, Charlotte, North Carolina
2. **Brenda Schetnan**, RN and Sierra Woods writer
3. **Anna Marie Jaworski**, Writer, publisher, speaker, and Internet talk radio host on VoiceAmerica! Her radio show, Heart to Heart With Anna: From My Heart to Yours, airs on the Health & Wellness channel. babyheartspress.com and congenitalheartdefects.com
4. **Tammye McDuff,** Your Wellness Guide, *Embrace ~ Marvel ~ Believe* tammye.mcduff@gmail.com, 714.471.5779 tammyedunn.moonfruit.com
5. **Karen Seeberg,** Spiritual Guidance Counselor See story on her near death experience on her site: livelovelaughmore.com vow2allow@yahoo.com
6. **Paula Sears,** Please see a site we've put up for Paula to help raise funds for new artificial legs and fingers. She could really use your help. She needs in order of importance:
    1. Most important is new sockets with all parts especially below knee side. Below knee cost is 3,927. Above knee cost is 6,495.
    2. New microprocessor knee for left leg—cost is 20,156.
    3. Cosmetic covers on legs. Total cost is 1,287.
    4. New feet. Total cost for 2 new top of the line feet is 6,122
    5. Cosmetic hand is between 5-10,000

Total cost is around $42,987 to $47,987.

Please help Paula get better artificial legs and hand. Donate at: gfwd.at/1ebaTsv

7. **Lawrence D. Elliott**, Author, *Chicken Soup for the Soul* and the Huffington Post contributor. Originally from San Diego, California, he lives

in Bensheim, Germany. lawrenceelliott.com
8. **Patrik Hutzel**, intensivecareathome.com.au and intensivecarehotline.com
9. **Ayn Cates Sullivan**, Ph.D. Award winning author. Her Sparkle stories are fairytales for children of all ages, addressing the way the Light changes lives. ayncatessullivan.com
10. **Michael W. Perry**, Author of *Hospital Gowns and Other Embarrassments: A Teen Girl's Guide to Hospitals* and *My Nights with Leukemia: Caring for Children with Leukemia.*InklingBooks.com
11. **Suzanne B. Quinn,** Lawyer, quinnlaw.ca, Suzanne's experience as a lawyer has provided unique insight into life situations and circumstances of extreme hardship. Her insights, counseling, and her personal journey have inspired her to provide practical guidance in transforming one's life.
12. **Jessica Mast,** Author of *The Call of a Caregiver: Finding Comfort, Pursuing Purpose.* She wrote it for people to see that they're not alone in what they are going through, and how no situation is hopeless. JessicaMMast.com
13. **Grace Dunklee Cohen,** Anthorne Group PR Mobile: 603-748-0085, Office: 603-428-6649, eMail: gcohen@anthorne.com
14. **GiveForward** provides personalized online fundraising pages to help with medical bills, and is one of the easiest ways to support a loved one in need. GiveForward.com, info@giveforward.com
15a. **Laura Ellison Cook**, Charlotte, North Carolina
15b. **Kevin Strauss, M.E.,** Founder and President - FamilyeJournal.com - Bringing Families Closer Together - Like us on Facebook.com/familyejournal - FREE to register, or fee-based when added to your organization's mental and emotional wellness program. Join FamilyeJournal today and FEEL the connection!
16. TakeThemAMeal.com is a free online tool that simplifies the process of coordinating meals so your time and energy can be spent caring for loved ones. Visit at www.takethemameal.com and on Facebook: www.facebook.com/takethemameal
17. **Helen Ashley**, Sydney based artist, mum and creator of ColourMeArt. The brand encourages creative kids to enjoy colour any grey day. colourmeart.com
18. Edna Ma, MD, Board Certified Anesthesiologist, creator of BareEASE, prep-kit for ouchless bikini waxing. BareEase.com
19. **Walter Meyer**, co-creator of Gam3rCon. Author of the award-winning novel, *Rounding Third.*
20. **Ruth Wilkes**, Author of the funtastic, children's book, *Dancing Fruit Put on a Show!* Kids go bananas over this fun story and also learn

all about fruit. DancingFruitBook.com
(She edits and helps with all my books tremendously. Thanks!)

21a. **Yolonda Brinkley** is a marketing communications professional specializing in events, public relations & lifestyle management. Visit http://youtu.be/24jIcFDCF2A to learn more, and email ybrinkley @hotmail.com to schedule a complimentary consultation.

21b. **David Andrew Lloyd**, Screenwriter, Author of *Instant Screenplay* available on Amazon. iknowfunny@aol.com (Editor of this book, who did an amazing job editing. Thanks.)

25. **Janet Miserandino,** butyoudontlooksick.com Author of *Disaster Master Plan: Prepare or Despair - It's Your Choice*

26. **Judy Logue Gibbons**, Illinois Realtor, Hunter's Fairway Sotheby's International Realty JudyGibbonsProperties.com Call 847.274.4983.

27a. **Mary & Autumn Sullivan,** Mother/Daughter authors of, *If I Had a Daddy* and *If We Were Best Friends.* Msmary726@aol.com

27b. **Lorelei A. Hill, B.A., B.Ed.**, Wellness/Happiness Coach, Soul Healing. Cardiac/Transplant Transition Mentor and Advisor. To book your Skype, Telephone, or In-Clinic Consultation call 519 832 8293, or email:yvonne@angelthinking.com

28. Personal experiences motivated Karen Curtiss' handbook on avoiding hospital hazards SafeAndSoundBooks.com

29. **Karen Palmer,** Founder and CEO Eco Angels, karensyv@yahoo.com | positivelypetsandkids.com

30. **Susan "Chef Teton" Campbell**, See this 68 year-old in a bikini at SusanTetonCampbell.com and you'll see why she's living proof her anti-aging food plan works!

31. **Ronald Kaufman**, Seminar Leader/Executive Coach, "Presentation Skills," "Negotiation," "Job Interviewing," and "Goal Setting/Motivation."Author of *Anatomy of Success.* anatomyofsuccess.com

34. **Lisa Gorman,** Lisa G Communication, lisagcommunication.com.au Daughter of 'Albert' John Winspear – who I'll love and cherish always.

35. **Alice Mosdell**, Editor-in-Chief, Goofy Guru Publishing, goofyguru.com

36. **Lara Fabans,** Online Marketing Consultant, lodestone-cs.com, Twitter: @larajf LinkedIn: linkedin.com/in/larafabans/

38a. **Devon Greene,** Caregiver, Newport Beach, CA

38b. **Laura Ellison Cook**, Charlotte, North Carolina

39. **http://goldilocksanesthesiafoundation.org/** Their mission is to educate Americas about the public health risk of too much anesthesia, and the value of direct brain activity monitors to avoid this risk.

40a. **Tina Mosetis**, Mosetis Marketing/Public Relations, Top NYC Public Relations firm for commercial and non-profit organizations. Over

25 year of experience. Mosetis PR will put the media spotlight on your business. MosetisPR.com Telephone: 516-487-5866

40b. **Angil Tarach-Ritchey RN, GCM**, Eldercare Expert, Speaker, Consultant, and Best-Selling and Award Winning Author of *Behind the Old Face: Aging in America and the Coming Elder Boom* with over 33 years in eldercare and advocacy, and has lived with chronic illness since 2003. Learn more and get a free 22 page mini-media preview eBook (M2eBook)behindtheoldface.com/?page_id=6

41. **D. Nikki Wheeler,** Sr. Manager, Global Communications, Terumo BCT

42. **Janet Collins Jordan,** Fort Lauderdale, FL tsjjordan@aol.com

43. **Jonathan Steele**, RN, Holistic nurse using natural treatments to improve health. He's the web host of WaterCures.org and Nurse-Jon.com. He specializes in, and lectures, around the world on holistic health management.

My water cures site is totally free, nothing for sale, no ads. It is my way of giving back to the US since everyone's taxes paid for my RN degree.

44. **Karen Weideman,** Teacher, blogger.thethriftymommy.com, twitter.com/thriftymommy, pinterest.com/thethriftymommy

45. **Katie Schwartz**, CCC-SLP, 2013 President, Corporate Speech Pathology Network BusinessSpeechImprovement.com, linkedin.com/profile/view?id=5764884&trk=tab_pro

46. **Elaine Wilkes.** See her researched favorites including health products, audios, books, and more at ElaineWilkes.com

47a. In honor of Tad and Bobbie Duncan, two of the best people in my little world. **Sharna Alt,** Redmond, WA.

47b. **Karen and Leslie, The Hug Sisters.** For more awesome ways to help someone who is sick, visit www.feelthehugs.com where our online store can send a perfect gift of a HUG. Join the hug movement on Facebook @ www.facebook.com/Feelthehugs

47c. **Natasha Carmon,** Author of *Poisonous Crimes of Passion, Highly Favored By Dog? God* highlyfavoredbdg.com, facebook.com/ favored-carma, favorredcarma@wordpress.com

47d. **Michael Laramee,** Co-Founder, mealTrain.commichael@ mealtrain.com, facebook.com/mealtrain, LinkedIn: /in/michaellaramee

47e. **Pamela Layton McMurtry**, Mom, artist and author of *A Harvest and Halloween Handbook,* amzn.to/18ADwWN,

Facebook: facebook.com/PamelaLaytonMcMurtry, pammcmurtry.com

48. **Brenda Schetnan,** RN and Sierra Woods writer.

49. **Katie Strand**, singer & filmmaker. Co-Founder of CHI Worldwide, a comprehensively sustainable wellness center & community, similar

to an eco village, in development. Co-Authored: *What Women Never Tell You.* chiworldwide.org, katiestrandworld.blogspot.com

50a. Mary McQueen and Luigi the Lovebird, Hand and Beak Cards for Kids www.handandbeak.com, @LuigiLovebird, ***Awesome Offer!*** **20% discount for readers of this book! Use coupon code:** AwesomeLuigi

50b. **Josephine Bila**, M.S.W., is an emotional wellness coach, motivational speaker, and expert patient consultant to the US Food and Drug Administration. Go to josephinebila.com/wilkes to receive a special gift for Elaine Wilkes fans. Connect with Josephine on
Facebook: fb.me/josephinebilafan and Twitter: @josephinebila

50d. **Ms. Crystal E Zobel**, Philanthropic Entrepreneur

50e. **Cherry-Ann Carew,** Award Finalist and Bestselling Author Cherry-Ann Carew | Book Coach | Developmental Editor | Founder of Writetastic Solutions helps aspiring writers to write, publish and market their books. ***Awesome Offer!*** Use Coupon Code: POWERWRITE101 to save 40% off her coaching program at: bit.ly/1dtc0zL and go here: bit.ly/1aP8MsI for free gifts.

51. **Stel Fines**, Inner Bonding Facilitator, innerbonding.com

Therapy Dog Sites

51a. **Therapy Dogs Inc.**, 877-843-7363, therapydogs.com Other info pertaining to contact info is therapydogsin@qwestoffice.net

51b. **Therapy Dogs International**, tdi-dog.org,
Phone: (973) 252-9800, E-mail: tdi@gti.net

51c. **Pet Partners**, petpartners.org, Phone: (425) 679-5500.

51d. **Bright and Beautiful Therapy Dogs**, golden-dogs.org, Phone: 888-PET-5770

54. **Michele Martin**, Dog sitter in Santa Monica, CA. I love pet sitting and taking great care of other people's precious animals - it is my calling - love, Michele funnycatwoman@mac.com

55. **Dr David Jockers**, Maximized Living Doctor and author of *Super Charge Your Brain.* You can find out more world-class health strategies at DrJockers.com

56. **Lorraine Holmes Milton**, M.S.,M.A., Veteran, Inventor. Author of *Disaster Master Plan: Prepare or Despair - It's Your Choice.* disastermasteru.com, Twitter:@lomilt

57. **Lily Hills** is a former compulsive overeater turned "Permanent and Pleasurable Weight Loss Coach" and Host Spark people Radio - #1 Health/Diet Site in America with over 15 million members. Lily is also the author of the award winning book, *The Body Love Manual- How to Love the Body You Have As You Create the Body You Want* and the founder of the online "getting over overeating" training ~ MasterYourMindMasterYourWeight.com.

For 3 FREE trainings on three things you MUST master to lose weight WITHOUT dieting go to LilyHills.com

58a. **Edna Ma, MD,** Board Certified Anesthesiologist, creator of BareEASE, prep-kit for ouchless bikini waxing. BareEase.com

58b. **Kimberly Friddle** is a public speaker who offers hope for those dealing with difficult medical diagnoses through her blog at thebrazenoptiist.comkimberly@kfcommunications.com

59. **April Dawn Ricchuito**. mental-makeup.com, verbalvandal-ism.com

60. **Kathy A. Eubanks**, Speaker and author of *When It's You Against Them*. KathyEubanks.com

61. **Jan Harvey** is an Artist living in The Cotswolds, England. To see her paintings please visit janharveyartist.co.uk

62. **Jan Harvey** runs The Wychwood Creative Workshops for the New, the Nervous and the Rusty! The courses, led by professionals and based in The Cotswolds, England, include photography, life drawing, yoga, public speaking, glass, writing and jewelry. Accommodation can be organized. Visit thewychwoodworkshops.co.uk

63. **Nancy D. Butler**, CFP®, CDFA™, CLTC, Professional national speaker, Entrepreneur, Award winning writer, and Business coach Author of *Above All Else, Success in Life and Business.* 860-444-0535, aboveallelse.org

64. **Allen Klein**, MA, CSP Award-winning professional speaker, Life-time Achievement Award recipient from the Association for Applied and Therapeutic Humor, Certified Speaking Professional from the National Speaker's Association. Author of *The Healing Power of Humor, Learning to Laugh When You Feel Like Crying*, and *The Art of Living Joyfully*. allenklein.com

65. **Giovina Taraschi**. facebook.com/giovina.taraschi, linkedin.com/pub/giovina-taraschi/2/8a3/5ba/, tunbridgepublishing.com

66. **Roberta Dehman Hershon**, Executive Director of Hope in Bloom—changing the landscape for breast cancer patients one garden at a time. hopeinbloom.org, facebook.com/pages/Hope-in-Bloom-Inc/78708347072

67. **Ann Bass**, CRTS, alightermove.com, abass@alightermove.com

68. **Steve Chard. Buyers of Elaine Wilkes' Books get 30% off anything @ YWPD.net** (email for reg price quote first). schard@ywpd.net Web design, marketing, & promotion. (Yes, that includes search engines.) FREE 2 page static websites for charities.

69. **Bridget Sims Lewis** from Dallas, TX

70. **Walter Meyer.** Co-Creator, Gam3rCon, Anti-bullying expert. For more information visit waltergmeyer.com

71. **Denise Taylor**, Speaker, author. Wacky Wednesday:www.weGETto.org. Instagram, username weGETto. Would consider it a great blessing if readers would start celebrating Wacky Wednesdays and spreading the cheer. A cheerful heart is like medicine. With Increasing Gratitude Every Day. weGETto.org,facebook.com/weGETto

72. **Andrea Sholer**, Real-Life-Law-of-Attraction.com Promoting the philosophy that the path to success in the life of your dreams is to be intentionally optimistic, develop possibility thinking, and focus on what you DO want (rather than on fears of what you don't want coming to pas

73. ertified Orthopedic Surgeon

gin.com,

lanager, The Soho Loft

any helping firms adver-

to get free newsletter

/visit/lisaguest

ert, Author, Speak-

are, Medicaid and

advice, informa-

Well Within:

m/ consulta-

onsultation to

fulfilled and empo-

ger of Bio Revive and Direc-

dysplasia resource site.

MT, RMP, Licensed Massage Therapist,

Soc ook, Illinois

78c. **Juliette,** Aesthetician, aestheticsbyjuliette.com, info@aestheticsbyjuliette.com. Offers services at no charge to cancer patients. Glen Ellyn, Illinois.

80a. **Eileen Roth,** Productivity Expert, author of Organizing For Dummies®, and owner of Everything in its Place® helps you be more productive so you have time to enjoy your life. Get notified of blog updates by signing up on her website: www.everythinginitsplace.net or contact Eileen at speaker@everythinginitsplace.net for more information.

80b. **Edna Ma**, MD, Board Certified Anesthesiologist, creator of BareEASE, prep-kit for ouchless bikini waxing. BareEase.com

80c. **Vickie Oldham**an Assistant Vice President of Communications in higher educations developed the "Looking for Angola" project that connectsresidents to scholars searching for archaeological evidence of a forgotten1800's Black Seminole settlement, lookingforangola.org or vjoldham@aol.com

81. **Healing Touch International, Inc.,** 303-989-7982

82. **Kim Westrope** lives in Sun City, CA. where she works as an Office Manager, and writes in her spare time. "I am so grateful to be a part of this project. I hope these stories will uplift, encourage, and inspire."

83. **Leslie Sloane**, Alchemist/Colour Metaphysician / Creator of Auracle's Colour Therapy. Author of *Auracle's Colour Therapy: The Power of Love Through Colour*, and *The Auracle: A Simple Guide To A Personal Awakening Card Deck* (With Healing Images & Mandalas). auraclescolourtherapy.com

85. **Dr. Jeanette Gallagher, ND**, Naturopathic Physician, patient/healthcare advocate, radio host. drjeanettegallagher.com and outoftheboxhealthcare.com

86. **Darren Hardy.** Publisher and editorial director of *SUCCESS magazine*. Blog: http://darrenhardy.success.com/about/

87. **Annette Langer,** Author/Speaker/Humorist, employs humor to temper somber topics. Visit AnnetteLanger.com to learn about her books, *Healing Through Humor: Change Your Focus, Change Your Life!* and *A Funny Thing Happened on My Way to the World: Diary of a Fearless Travel Agent.*

87b. **Dr. Jeffrey Ptak, DC, MA,** Chiropractor. Teaching health and wellness thru the Maximized Living 5 Essentials. West Los Angeles, CA, 310-473-7991, ptakchiropractic.com, drjeffreyptak@gmail.com

88a. **Marie Davis and Margaret Hultz**, Wickedly Sisters, App Developers. *Spoon and the Moon*, top-selling app on Amazon, Gold Medal Winner. This wildly imaginative story full of humor, a twinge of tenderness, and a heaping of unexpected turns has won several prestigious awards.

AwesomeOffer! We would like to offer your readers a free copy of our app, if they will email us at spoonandthemoon@yahoo.com — put in the subject line: Free Awesome Book -- we can then get them a copy once we know the device they use.

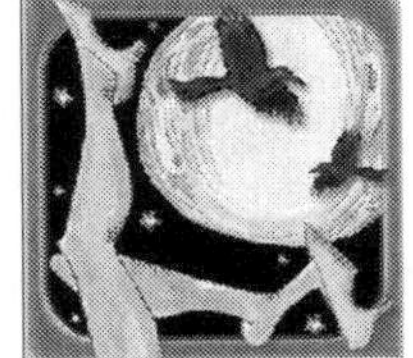

88b. **Katie Strand**, singer & filmmaker. Co-Founder of CHI Worldwide, a comprehensively sustainable wellness center & community, similar to an ecovillage, in development. Co-

Authored: *What Women Never Tell You.*
chiworldwide.org, katiestrandworld.blogspot.com

88c. **Lara Fabans,** Online Marketing Consultant, lodestone-cs.com, Twitter: @larajf LinkedIn: linkedin.com/in/larafabans/

89. **Claudia M. Seggel**, Founder of Claudia's Cools Hats, 561-715-4076 claudia@claudiascoolhats.com, claudiascoolhats.com

Awesome Offer! Use the coupon code "awesome" for a discount.

90. **Brad Butcher**, Rotary Club of Rocks Riverside facebook.com/Rotary.BrisbaneRocksRiverside

91. ***Awesome Offer!*** UPPERCASES is dedicated to comforting people everywhere, and will extend free personalization ($4 value) to anyone who mentions this book when ordering.

Find us at uppercases.com and facebook.com / uppercases. Contact us at uppercases@twc.com or (502)403-5655.

92a. **Brenda Jones,** hugwraps@verizon.net, hugwraps.org

92b. **P.J.Salvage Pajamas**, info@pjsalvage.com, pjsalvage.com

93. My family has been in the Kitchen & Bath Industry for 3 generations. In IL, WI or MN if you are in need of built-in/custom cabinetry for your home, kindly visit us at **GreenfieldCabinetry.com**, 312.644.4466. With thanks to Elaine for this unique book to share my memory in, **Karla (Krengel) Hood.**

94. **Melanie Koerperich**, milrichassociates.com We can provide virtual concierge services for you or your loved ones.

95a. **Laura Ellison Cook**, Charlotte, North Carolina

95b. **Joy Johnston,** writer. joyjohnston.writer@gmail.com, memories-project.com

96. **Randy Peyser** is the author of *Crappy to Happy, The Power of Miracle Thinking*, and the upcoming books, *The Little Book of Big Epiphanies*, and *Bald Courage*. For her *"Create Miracles"* text and audio messages delivered to your cell phone or iPad:
everalive.us/collections/frontpage/products/miraclethinking

97. **Barbara Gabogrecan,** Artist and author. Drouin, Victoria. GabogrecanStrokeRecovery.com, SilkPaintingByGabogrecan.com

98. **Charles Breitweiser,** Motivational speaker, author

99. From **Elaine Wilkes.** See her researched favorites including health products, audios, books, and more at ElaineWilkes.com

99. (Enemas). **Matt Storey**, Certified nutritionist and consultant to healthcare practitioners looking to integrate holistic protocols into their practice. He has15+ years experience. **Premier Research Labs** | Dial +1 800.325.7734 Ext. 2505, matt@prlabs.com| prlabs.com

100. **Laura Ellison Cook**, Charlotte, North Carolina

Thanks to these awesome designers!

Book interior layout:
Access Ideas
access.ideas@yahoo.com

Front cover design:
Jake Muelle
jakemuelle@gmail.com

Back cover design:
Karolin Frimodig
karolinfrimodig@hotmail.com

Sharad Poddar and **Ruchi**
of BrainDesk.net
for their terrific assistance.

Awesome Editors:

Ruth Wilkes and **David Lloyd**

About the Author
Elaine Wilkes, PhD

Elaine has a Ph.D. in naturopathy (alternative medicine), graduating with honors, and a master's degree in psychology. These synergistically work together to help the body-mind-soul connection.

Elaine has appeared as an expert on *CNN Headline News, E Entertainment* TV, *Kid's Talk* TV, along with being interviewed for documentaries, and is quoted in publications such as *The Chicago Tribune, Alternative Medicine, Forbes,* and *Women's World* magazines to name a few.

Elaine has a professional acting background. She was under contract with NBC, and has appeared in numerous television shows and movies with the top "A" list actors and directors such as Bruce Willis, Madonna, Courtney Cox, Larry Hagman, Billy Zane, Mark Harmon, Jay Leno, Ted Danson, Patrick Duffy, John Hughes, Blake Edwards, and many more! She's also appeared in more than 75 TV commercials.

She's also a K.R.I. certified instructor of meditation and yoga. Plus, she's an accredited LEED™ (Leadership in Energy and Environmental Design) professional.

See udemy.com and search for Elaine Wilkes, to see the courses she's created.

About Elaine's Award-Winning Book, Nature's Secret Messages

Elaine's award-winning book, *Nature's Secret Messages: Hidden in Plain Sight*, (Hay House Publishing) received the highly coveted *Publishers Weekly* rare star recommendation.

Elaine shares innovative ways of dealing with life by revealing nature's secrets.

"This book is a page-turner—endlessly fascinating, totally compelling, and incredibly informative. I could not put it down.

– Rory Freedman,
Co-Author of *New York Times* best seller *Skinny Bitch*

"With a dash of tongue-in-cheek cheer, actress and PhD-carrying naturopath Wilkes offers a thorough, clear-cut and well-illustrated introduction to holistic medicine, natural eating and the benefits of mindfulness."

–Publishers Weekly

Paperback:
http://amzn.to/13OYO1T

Kindle:
http://amzn.to/13Jo2Cf

Now available for the iPad:
http://bit.ly/13JLJMV

Please visit Elaine's websites for a list of her favorite health products and services:

"As a naturopath and nutritionist I'm dedicated to helping people stay healthy. I've gathered my list from constant research, attending conventions, seminars, networking, reading and testing for what's the best (and usually closest to nature) out there."

–Elaine

Please see more awesome stuff on
Facebook.com/101Awesomethings,

or the

websites:
101AwesomeThings.com
http://www.ElaineWilkes.com

Put a Smile On a Sick Child's Face

When Bobbie Banana Splits His Pants

Laughter is the best medicine!

Elaine turned her mom's funtastic children's book, *Dancing Fruit Put on a Show!* into an interactive iPad version, with music, sound effects, a read-to-me feature, down on the farm video, and lots of laughs. What an awesome way to introduce kids to healthy fruit and fun!

It comes in hard cover, paperback, ebook, English, Spanish, and iPad versions. Children's book ages 3 - 8.

See: http://www.DancingFruitBook.com

Made in the USA
Lexington, KY
01 November 2014